"With *The Power of Failure*, Fran Tarkenton creates a motivating paradigm for entrepreneurs by showing that 'fail fast, fail cheap, succeed faster' is a mind-set as well as a practical and necessary approach to business. Fran was a great friend to our founder, Harland Stonecipher, and continues to be an invaluable partner to LegalShield, and someone to whom I turn for inspiration and counsel."

—**JEFF BELL**, CEO of LegalShield

"Having worked with Steven Jobs, Bill Gates, Michael Milken, Rupert Murdoch, Bob Iger, and Alex Gorsky, I consider myself the Forrest Gump of American business—certainly the luckiest guy on the planet. But I've never met a smarter, more intuitive, and more inventive CEO than Fran Tarkenton. The great Bear Bryant of Alabama said he always wanted an ideal in players: 'mobile, agile, and hostile.' He wanted Fran Tarkenton. And always will. Fran is in the Hall of Fame of Entrepreneurs."

—**SCOTT MILLER**, CEO of Core Strategy Group

"Fran's generosity and fierce commitment to learning shine through on every page of his latest book. Few entrepreneurs would ever dream of being so forthcoming with their struggles and failures, but Fran embraces every lick he's ever taken, both on the field and off, as opportunities to learn and grow. That generosity coupled with his no-nonsense storytelling are why this book will have such a positive impact on your personal and professional life."

—**BOLAND T. JONES**, Founder, Chairman, and CEO of PGi

"Fran Tarkenton made a remarkable transition from Hall of Fame quarterback to successful entrepreneur. In this engrossing book, he shares his football and business experience to make a compelling case that losing is the key to winning. I dare you not to stand up and cheer while reading it."

—**ADAM GRANT,** Wharton professor and *New York Times* bestselling author of *Give and Take*

"In his new book Fran Tarkenton brings to life the fact that failure is an immensely powerful fact of life and business. Fran is an exceptional mentor, business partner, and friend, and as I read this book I found his personal stories and candor around his struggles and failures deeply inspiring—I have no doubt they will hit home for every entrepreneur, business owner, and executive in personal and meaningful ways. Read this book and join the failure revolution—let the F-word set you free!"

—**MICHAEL J. PIRES,** Founder and Former CEO, HR411.com, and DVP, Business Development at ADP, LLC

"As a self-made founder, CEO, and entrepreneur with over thirty years in business and seven hundred franchises worldwide, I can honestly say that Fran offers sage advice in an open, honest, and very genuine way. Fran's insight and recommendations transcend traditional concepts and offer real-world solutions for leadership, managing and embracing change, and building a lasting business enterprise.

Failures in life and business can often times take a long time to see coming. Fran's ability to relate to his days on the field—where every successful play sets the team up one step closer to their goal of scoring and ultimately winning—is a valuable lesson in itself. I strongly recommend this book to anyone who is building or growing a business or who just wants to set themselves on a course to self-improvement and enrichment."

—**STEVEN GREENBAUM,** CEO and Founder,
PostNet International Franchise Corporation

"The very first time I met Fran, he exemplified one of the key lessons that I have learned in my business and personal life. A true leader focuses on making others better as a result of what they do—no more, no less. In that context, there really is very little difference between Fran as a Hall of Fame quarterback and Fran as a successful entrepreneur and teacher. In telling his story, he gives us all the permission we often need to take the failures we all frequently face and build on them—with a generousness of spirit and innate desire to learn that is always refreshing."

—**MALCOLM MCROBERTS,** Senior Vice President,
Small Business Services, Deluxe Corporation

"It is a widely held belief that doctors know hardly anything about the world of business. There is probably a fair amount of truth to that, but thankfully we are good learners as well. The man I have turned to for education over the years is Fran Tarkenton. Besides having enviable energy at seventy-five years old, he is a world-class explainer and teacher. In his latest book, he takes on the age-old concept of failure, and puts a muscular new spin on it.

Surely we all know real success hardly ever comes without real failure—but hearing the narrative from one of the greatest professional quarterbacks to play the game gives it a level of clarity and significance. I have had the good fortune of being able to call on Fran Tarkenton and benefit from his experience, judgment, and powerful wisdom. Now that wisdom is available to everyone by simply turning the page."

—**SANJAY GUPTA,** Assistant Professor of Neurosurgery, Emory University, and CNN Chief Medical Correspondent

THE POWER OF FAILURE

FRAN **TARKENTON**

THE**POWER** OF **FAILURE**

SUCCEEDING IN THE AGE OF INNOVATION

REGNERY
PUBLISHING
A Division of Salem Media Group

Regnery® is a registered trademark of Salem Communications Holding Corporation

Cataloging-in-Publication data on file with the Library of Congress

ISBN 978-1-62157-403-3

Published in the United States by
Regnery Publishing
A Division of Salem Media Group
300 New Jersey Ave NW
Washington, DC 20001
www.Regnery.com

Manufactured in the United States of America

10 9 8 7 6 5 4 3 2 1

Books are available in quantity for promotional or premium use. For information on discounts and terms, please visit our website: www.Regnery.com.

Distributed to the trade by
Perseus Distribution
250 West 57th Street
New York, NY 10107

This book is dedicated to Linda, my wife and partner for the past twenty-three years. She shares my passion for knowledge and has been a perfect partner in my quest for greater understanding. Linda has been more than just a great companion, she's used her personality and intellect to help me build and maintain a tremendous network of friends who share their own unique experiences with us and add to our invaluable repository of knowledge gained through trial and failure.

CONTENTS

FOREWORD

BY BENJAMIN AYERS
DEAN OF THE TERRY COLLEGE OF BUSINESS

"Power" is usually not the first word that comes to mind when we think of failure. Most of us have been programmed since early childhood not only to see failure as a negative, but to avoid it at all costs. Our entire culture—our movies, our novels, and certainly most self-help books—are filled with examples of how to "succeed." Failure is weakness, something to shake off, something to push into the past and try to forget.

Fran Tarkenton knows failure. That may sound funny to say about a Hall of Fame quarterback who played in three Super Bowls, has built a flourishing career in business, and meets almost any definition of "success" in life. But it's true. Fran Tarkenton knows failure. He has experienced it, he understands it, and he has learned a lot of very important lessons from it along the way.

Talking with Fran, you're inevitably struck by how open and transparent he is about his setbacks. The games he lost, the business ideas that fizzled, the great ideas that initially succeeded only to run into later obsolescence. Fran doesn't hide from these experiences. He never whitewashes mistakes, passes the blame, or runs from the truth.

In this, Fran's latest book, *The Power of Failure*, he explains the profound but fundamental concept of failure in a clear, personal, and entertaining way. When you read this book, you'll come away with the understanding that we can turn something we usually think of as a negative into something not only positive, but meaningful—and overwhelmingly generous.

That's because Fran understands not only the failures he has experienced in his own life, but just how important failure is for everyone. His insight—and, as he'll surely tell you, it's not an idea original to him—is that failure is not an undesirable outcome, but a necessary part of the innovation process. The two are inextricably linked; you cannot have one without the other. When our mistakes cause us to examine what we did wrong, then we learn something valuable. Failure becomes a gift—a gift of knowledge. When we run from mistakes and lock them away, the insights derived from analyzing those errors are never added into the process. It's only when we embrace our failures and learn from them that we can really make not just small steps, but great leaps forward.

Fran has never feared failure, and that, ironically, has been the key to his success. He has never been content with simply following the crowd and hoping for the best. Rather, he has embraced uncertainty and risks in pursuit of his goals.

In his NFL days, his goal was not just "to be a successful quarterback." If it had been, he would have played to fit the mold of what a "successful quarterback" looked like then. Instead, his goal was to make his teammates better, in order to give the team the best chance to win. With that goal in mind, he revolutionized the game of football as the first scrambling quarterback. He jumped into the unknown, despite the risk of failure, recognizing that he had found an innovative way to help his team.

Having a more meaningful goal that he connected with on a deep, personal level led to greater success, not only for himself, but for his teammates as well.

It has been the same for Fran in the business world. If his goals had been "to be a successful businessperson and make a lot of money," I think Fran would have done things quite differently than he did. He certainly wouldn't have taken the same chances. Instead, his mission, as he will tell anyone who asks, is to help other people and create value in their lives. That's a mission that requires taking risks. As a result, he has tried new things, looked for fresh solutions to problems, and worked hard to bring about "game changers," the big innovations that are revolutionary, not just evolutionary. And, perhaps counterintuitively, embracing the possibility of failure has made him more successful than he ever would have been by just chasing after success itself.

Now, in 2015, Fran is seventy-five years old. But the minute he starts talking, you experience the energy, drive, and passion of a man far younger than his years. He'll talk about his failures, but they are not a weight on his shoulders. Every new thing he tries, no matter the outcome, becomes fuel for his next effort. Even though he has achieved our society's vision of success, Fran is still going, because the mission of helping other people is never complete. There's always something else to try, something that might help a few more people, a little bit better. And whether it succeeds or fails, you can be sure that Fran will learn from it and try again.

Throughout his life, Fran Tarkenton has demonstrated that the important thing is to keep moving forward. That movement propels us to get out of our comfort zones and innovate, creating value for everyone. And, ultimately, that generosity, that act of creating and sharing value, is a true measure of success.

JOIN THE FAILURE REVOLUTION

In eighteen seasons with the NFL, I won more than I lost. But, like everyone else who plays professional football, I lost a lot. In far more years as an entrepreneur, I've achieved plenty of successes. Behind every one of them was a failure. Often more than one. Some of the failures were altogether mine, some involved others, but each affected me—sometimes painfully, but almost always usefully. In fact, I would not trade my failures for the world. They taught me what I needed to succeed.

The do-or-die line that Ed Harris, as NASA mission director Gene Kranz, delivers in Ron Howard's 1995 movie *Apollo 13* is so memorable that it has entered the American lexicon of business leadership: "Failure is not an option."

True. For today's entrepreneur, failure is not an *option*. It is a *fact of life*.

Welcome to what I call the "Age of Innovation and Failure," the warp-speed cycle of innovation-failure-innovation that is our Networked Information Economy. Today's accelerated technology and marketing cycles have exponentially increased both the opportunity and demand for entrepreneurial start-ups and the innovation they bring. Innovation—a torrent of new products and services—has, in turn, accelerated failure. In fact, success and failure are nothing more or less than moments in the same cycle.

In my experience, on the field, in the huddle, in the locker room, in the marketplace, in the venture capital meeting, and even at the cocktail party, almost no one is willing to talk about failure, its pain, its benefits, its inevitability. Most of us fear failure, disown it, deny it, or simply try to ignore it.

What we should be doing is talking about it, exploring it, embracing it, and squeezing out of it every priceless insight it offers.

Things *are* beginning to change—even if just barely. We are in the early days of a Failure Revolution, in which the business environment is finally starting to catch up to my personal embrace of failure as an opportunity to learn, improve, and win. The question for today's entrepreneurs and business leaders is whether to join the revolution or be kicked to the curb by it.

While learning from failure has always been a good business strategy, it is, in today's environment, an absolutely necessary one. I find myself—at seventy-five, old for a football player but (believe me) still young for an entrepreneur—the perfect fit for this new world. I want to share with you my experience, what I have learned, and what I am learning every day.

In the chapters that follow, I explore the success-failure-success cycle that parallels the innovate-fail-innovate rhythm found throughout today's business environment. It is a story based mostly on my life as an entrepreneur. It is the story I know best, and I believe it has a lot to say to other entrepreneurs, aspiring entrepreneurs, owners of small businesses, and those thinking of "going into business for themselves." But I hope that anyone in any business of any size will find value in this book.

I lay out my philosophy of lose fast and lose often to win long. I talk about the almighty value of using the F-word, of shattering illusions of perfection to achieve the reality of success, and of learning not to *avoid* mistakes but to start making *better* mistakes.

Most of this book is about change in a world of change. And believe me, change is key. But so are endurance and continuity. Technology drives, demands, and enables change. Markets are created, are reshaped, and sometimes vanish entirely. But people—customers, suppliers, employees, partners, and investors—are forever. Relationships will always be at the heart of business, and so I share what I know about the crucial necessity of putting people first, last, and middle in everything you do.

The products and services you offer, the means by which you reach your markets, and the markets themselves will all change and, these days, change quickly. In contrast, the culture you create for your business can and must last a long, long time. Culture is the single most important factor in determining success in life as well as business. This book will give you a head start on creating a culture built on kindness, willingness to help others, respect for differences, open-mindedness to new ideas and diverse attitudes, and—I'm not afraid of the word—love.

At the heart of a successful business culture is education—acquired not by accumulating facts and figures, but by reading everything and anything, talking to everyone, and exposing yourself to what others are doing and thinking. Knowledge created in this way really is power.

Success is a wonderful thing and a worthy objective. But we've all talked and heard enough about it by now. Failure is a gift, if you know how to accept and use it. *Reframe* failure within an open and generous business culture as venture, adventure, creation, creative destruction, and experimentation. Your vision will become action, and your actions will become reality. The elements of failure are also the elements of innovation, the Golden Ticket to success in today's business environment.

CHAPTER 1

FUELED BY FAILURE

CULTURE TRUMPS EVERYTHING

HITCH YOUR DRIVE TO KNOWLEDGE AND DISCIPLINE

CONTROL THE CONTROLLABLE, AND DON'T SWEAT THE REST

BUY A ONE-WAY TICKET

READ THE SIGNS

WHEN YOU *CAN* MAKE A DIFFERENCE, *MAKE A DIFFERENCE*

CULTIVATE AN ATTITUDE OF DESPERATION

GET INTO THE MOMENT AND STAY THERE

"YOU ARE NOT BEATEN UNTIL YOU ADMIT IT. HENCE, DON'T."

PROVE THEM WRONG

MAKE FAILURE THE FUEL THAT GETS YOU THERE

OWN THE LOSS

SHARE THE WEALTH: BE GENEROUS WITH FAILURE

BE BIG ON LEARNING, AND LET EVERYTHING INSPIRE YOU

JOIN THE FAILURE REVOLUTION

We were losing. It was Saturday, September 20, 1958, Georgia's season opener at Austin, Texas, my first game with the varsity team. We trailed the Longhorns 7 to 0 in the middle of the third quarter. Through two and a half quarters, we had not made a first down. All that time, I stood on the sideline next to Coach Wally Butts, watching us lose. I kept talking to him about Charley Britt, our starting quarterback. With Tommy Lewis—who, like Britt, was a year ahead of me—he was an outstanding talent. In fact, during their senior year in high school, Britt and Lewis were the top two quarterback prospects in the country.

"Charley looks tired. Let me give him a little breather, a little rest. Coach, put me in. Put me in for just one play."

For most of two and a half quarters, I repeated some variation of this plea, at times even tugging on the coach's sleeve, like a toddler. Butts did not flinch, did not blink, never acknowledged me in any way. I could have been talking to myself.

But then, at last, with our defense holding, Texas punted to us, and our guy made a fair catch on our own 5-yard line. This triggered the customary controlled chaos as our defensive team came off the field and our offense jogged out to take it. Players coming in, players going out, passing each other.

Wally Butts paid no attention to me at all, but I knew what was going through his head. I had quarterbacked my high school team, and, after a spectacular season my senior year, I turned down other offers and chose Georgia—even though the team already had those two outstanding quarterbacks. Friends and family warned me: "You'll never get to play." But I stuck to my choice.

Brooklyn Dodgers general manager Branch Rickey, who ended racial segregation in professional baseball when he brought Jackie Robinson to his team, once defined *luck* as "the residue of design." Maybe in going with Georgia—against all advice—I was demonstrating my determination to design *my* luck in a way that included the toughest of challenges. Maybe I wanted a merciless yardstick to let me measure how good I was or wasn't. Or maybe I was just convinced I was right. Whatever the reason, I and I alone had put *myself* on that Georgia team—and that put me on the sidelines. If choosing Georgia was a mistake, it was my mistake, and I had to own it. There was no one else to blame, not even Coach Butts. For him, Britt and Lewis figured as the go-to guys, while

I was an unknown quantity. As Butts saw it, I had plenty of time to prove myself—later.

But how could I possibly wait? My team was losing, and I felt confident I could make a difference. My team needed *me*. Now, right now—not next year. Coach Butts didn't flinch. What could I do? Keep tugging at his sleeve? I was the *third-team* quarterback, absolutely destined *not* to play. It made me desperate, which, it turned out, was a very good thing.

Our defense was coming off the field, the offense going onto it. In the chaos of moving bodies, I glanced toward our bench. There was Charley Britt, our starting quarterback, still sitting on the bench. Incredible! If for some reason someday I should ever have to write a book about him, I know just what I'd call it: *Get off the Bench*. In all my years in high school, college, and NFL football, I never sat on the bench. If I sat at all, it was on my helmet on the sideline. More often, I stood—on the sideline, right next to the coach. That's where I could learn something. That's where I could make myself ready.

I didn't calculate. I didn't think. The sight of Charley just sitting there put my feet into motion long before my brain started thinking....

CULTURE TRUMPS EVERYTHING

I'll give you the rest of the story of September 20, 1958, before this chapter ends, I promise. But let me tell you right now that the day had both consequences and a backstory. The consequences, as you'll see, play a big part in the rest of this book. The backstory—well, I suppose it is the whole of my young life leading up to that day.

I was born in Richmond, Virginia, but my family moved to Washington, D.C., when I was just five. For some time, we lived not far from the Old Soldiers' Home, in a small two-story house at 4100 5th Street NW. It was a working-class neighborhood of narrow streets and even narrower alleys, one of which ran behind our house. My brother Dallas and I and all of our friends played touch football in that alley, an unglamorous "field" that turned out to be a pretty good place to develop football skills. It gave us no room for error—literally. It was no easy feat to throw a pass fast, hard, and right on the button down a corridor just one car length wide or to go long without getting touched or tumbling headlong over a minefield of garbage cans.

Along with the skills, I grew an intense passion for the game. I'm told there are people who get really good at something without feeling much joy in whatever it may be—good doctors who have no great passion for medicine, fine musicians who feel little enthusiasm for music. I've never met any of them myself. All the masters of their craft I've ever encountered personally, in sports, business, science, the entertainment world, you name it, have been intensely passionate. That's also how it's always been with me.

In that alley, I first pretended to be Sammy Baugh, the Redskins great, but then University of Maryland quarterback Jack Scarbath became my idol. In fact, he continued to hold a place in my heart and imagination throughout my career. He was number 10, and so I would be, when I played for my high school team, for the Georgia Bulldogs, for the Minnesota Vikings, and for the New York Giants. For Dallas and me, alley football was our fantasy football, but we always played out the fantasy in a hard, narrow, and unyielding physical reality. Whatever that taught me about playing the game, it taught me even more about putting everything you've got into your passions and your dreams as you take reality head-on.

When I was ten, my family moved again, this time to Athens, Georgia, home of the University of Georgia. Dad was pursuing his dream of earning a doctorate in religion and education. It was a dream as remarkable as any I had at ten or would ever have as an adult. Dad combined a calling as a Pentecostal preacher with a vocation as a real estate entrepreneur. I'm not talking Donald Trump here. My father grew up in the rough Berkley neighborhood of Norfolk, Virginia. His policeman father was killed when Dad was nine or ten, and his mother died about five years later, leaving the fifteen-year-old to raise his younger sister. I don't have to tell you that Dad was poor. That much is obvious. But he always worked, got a low-cost, faith-based education at Holmes Bible College in Greenville, South Carolina, started preaching, and used what little money was left over to buy houses and rent them out at a profit sufficient to support three children. My mom contributed to our slim treasury by cleaning rooms, and while we didn't have much, we never went hungry, we always had decent clothes, and we were never without a roof over our heads. For me, my parents' example was a lifelong lesson in the most fundamental fundamentals of entrepreneurship. Dad pursued his two passions—religion and education—while always finding ways to keep us fed, clothed, and housed. He never put our welfare on the line. He might have been a preacher, but he never preached to us. He walked the walk. He modeled the morality he wanted us to develop for ourselves. He never told us what to be, but his example unmistakably communicated that he wanted *us* to be the best *we* could be.

To this day, I never preach. I'm a full-on serial entrepreneur, but I really don't believe in selling. I don't want to sell anybody anything. I don't want to convert anybody into anything—not with this book and not with any of my businesses. The "mission statement" of this book is the same as the mission statement of every business I've ever built: I want to help my readers, my customers, my employees, my partners—everyone I work with—to be the best they can be. Back in high school, college, and NFL football, it was all about the team, all about each other and having each other's back. Nobody had to give us these priorities. We knew them instinctively. It's in the DNA of football players. We're not playing golf. Football is a team sport. I couldn't throw a pass flat on my back. I needed guards and tackles to block for me and tight ends and receivers to catch. For me, football culture was always a team culture. We needed each other if we wanted a chance to be successful, and the whole reason to play a sport is to be successful. So I wanted to help my team-mates be the best *they* could be so that *we* could be the best team we could be.

In fact, I loved my teammates. We were dependent on one another, and we played for each other. It was the only chance we had to win, and, make no mistake, every team I was on wanted to win. My role model for this feeling, attitude, and approach was my dad, who created—to use a business term—a very special *culture* in my family. It was a culture of respect, transparency, and kindness, of openness to people as they are. We didn't yell and scream in my family. Nobody got cussed out, belittled, or shamed. At the time, of course, I didn't know this was a "culture." It was just my family. But it is how I learned—from a father who treated us all with respect, who loved us, and who quietly demanded discipline and hard work from us. He would not let us settle for being lazy, for being late, for just getting by in school. He drew out our best and made us want to deliver our best.

My best? Actually, I have never felt that I achieved it. Driven as I always was, my "best" always became better. So I never reached "my best"—thank goodness. We were a strong, loving family, always helping each other. Family became the foundation for everything I would build as an adult in sports and in business. Culture trumps everything else in how you run your business and how you live your life. It is easier for any enterprise to survive a flawed business plan than a flawed culture.

HITCH YOUR DRIVE TO KNOWLEDGE AND DISCIPLINE

So my dad, orphaned early in life, growing up dirt poor, went on to earn the highest academic degree a great university had to offer. Remarkable! And yet it really happened. I saw it, lived it, and learned from it. While I do love to learn—from everything I do and from everyone I meet—I have to confess that I didn't share Dad's passion for school. I made good grades, but I was bored in the classroom. For me, going to class was something you had to do in order to play team sports. When I started at Athens High School (today called Clarke Central High School), I was the co-starting quarterback on the football team as a thirteen-year-old freshman, a starter and leading scorer on the basketball team as a fourteen-year-old freshman (we went to the state playoffs), and the number one pitcher and shortstop on the baseball team (which went to the North Georgia championship).

Many people said I was better at basketball and baseball than at football. I was even drafted in baseball by the Detroit Tigers! But I had two extraordinary coaches, Weyman Sellers, my football coach, and Billy Henderson, a baseball coach who also was my backfield coach. They were the most demanding coaches I ever played for. No other coach, not in college and not in the NFL, required more from their players than they did. Sellers and Henderson made the game of football so challenging that I couldn't think about doing anything else. And by "challenging," I most definitely do not mean *fun*. With them, it was always about physical and mental conditioning instilled through relentless drill: longer practices, harder practices than anything in college or pro football. Sellers yelled a lot. I didn't like that then, and I don't like it now. It is *despite* his reliance on intimidation, not because of it, that Coach Sellers was able to help me build a foundation of fundamentals and discipline that has served me not only in the NFL, but in my life as an entrepreneur.

Along with Henderson, Sellers imparted knowledge and demanded discipline. The two men made me learn how to play quarterback the right way—the fundamentals, the footwork, the reading of defenses, the proper way to throw, the proper way to play. It was practice, practice, practice, redundancy, redundancy, redundancy. Games? They were easy after all that. What I gained was the lifelong habit, on the field and in the office, of paying attention to every detail, working hard, and being a playmaker: a person who gets things done, who completes passes, who makes the right handoff, who makes the right read of the defense, who makes the right run, and who does it all *now*. Urgently.

I gulped it all down, took it all in, but neither of these men could have given me the drive to excel. I had to discover that within myself and for myself. Everyone has to. Whether playing pro ball or starting, running, and growing your own company, there is no substitute for relentless inner drive hitched to hard-won knowledge and hard-earned discipline.

Sellers and Henderson made Athens football so tough that few of my classmates wanted to join the team. And as much as even I hated all the hollering and the browbeating, the two of them undeniably did something right. In 1955, we won the Georgia State High School Championship.

Seeing as we had no bench to speak of—just twenty-one players on the entire team roster, with no B squad, no junior varsity team, and no freshman team—that victory should have been impossible, especially going up against Valdosta, which was (and remains today) the state's high school powerhouse. The Valdosta football program began in 1913. In 2012, its nearly hundred-year record stood at 891 wins, 216 losses, and 34 ties, with 41 regional, 23 state, and 6 national championships. Yet we managed to beat Valdosta for the 1955 championship 41 to 30.

For me, the 1955 championship was also special for urgent personal reasons. At fifteen, during my junior year, we had a tackling drill in which I separated my shoulder. I probably should not have played again until my shoulder had healed, but I didn't think about not playing. I just kept playing. Before the injury, I could throw a football 75 yards, no problem. After it, for the rest of the season, I couldn't throw more than 10 yards. Instead of standing down, however, I was determined to become the greatest ball handler who ever lived—hiding the ball, handing it off. I'd never been much of a running quarterback—quarterbacks didn't run much in that era, not in high school or college—but I did have the instincts of what we today call scrambling: avoiding the pass rush and buying time to throw a pass. My injury gave me an urgent need to develop those instincts.

Most of all, I studied and practiced and became an outstanding field general. As I built more experience calling plays, I learned how to study the enemy, their habits, strengths, and weaknesses. I spent hours and hours with Weyman Sellers and Billy Henderson studying films of what our opponents were doing with their defense. In this way, I was able to plan to counter each and every thing they might throw at us. As a result, I was rarely surprised by anything an opponent did in a game. For me, it was a series of early lessons in innovation and creativity that would continue to serve me long after I retired from football.

It was all because I had to find a way to help my team win without passing the football. I got hurt the third week of a ten-week season, but we still ended up beating Valdosta. In that entire championship game, I threw a single pass, which was incomplete. Instead of throwing, I ran the ball and field-generaled the team. Our victory was a total team triumph, the product of solid fundamentals, relentless conditioning, and absolute discipline combined with a selfless teamwork ethic. If anything, my injury forced me to be even more of a team player than I already was, and I also learned that there was no adversity that could keep me down.

CONTROL THE CONTROLLABLE, AND DON'T SWEAT THE REST

In the beginning, my bad shoulder made me worry that my high school football career would be cut short and that I'd never get onto a college team, let alone into professional football. Soon, however, useless worry morphed into invaluable desperation. I simply became that much more determined to play football, and not just football, but great football. Just about everybody sees desperation as a negative. The emotional state of the truly pathetic, it seems to most something to be shed and shunned. But not to me. I embraced my desperation, let it drive me, pushing me in directions I never thought of before—like developing a running game and doing everything I could to help my teammates perform at their highest levels. With a bad shoulder, what other choice did I have? Even as a pro, I never threw longer than 55 yards. I had to keep improving all my compensating skills. I ended up, in pro football, with all the records for passing and for rushing yards by a quarterback. I learned to use my legs to buy time to throw.

All of this took practice. But the one thing I never practiced was "how to win." I couldn't do that, and, actually, nobody can. I didn't think *win* or *lose*. I thought about making plays, making first downs, getting my teammates in position to get us first downs so that we could make touchdowns. I learned early on that you have no control over the ultimate outcome of a game any more than you have control over an injury. If you can't control something, why sweat it? Why let it distract you from what you *can* control?

In fact, I never thought about my shoulder as a handicap. It was just something I was dealt. I no more envied a player whose shoulder was perfectly sound than I envied quarterbacks who were bigger, faster, or stronger than I was. If someone asked me, "Wouldn't it be nice to be a six-foot-four quarterback?" I would answer, "No. I never thought being a six-foot quarterback was a handicap." I could not control my DNA, and I never envied anybody else's DNA. I did, however, do everything I could to gain and develop skills that would make me the best *I* could be. Fortunately, *my* best proved to be a moving target. So I just kept getting better.

None of this guaranteed a win. Such a guarantee was beyond my control, but it was well within my ability to influence. To use a bit of business-speak, each of these details was *actionable*, and each put us in a better position to win, ratcheting up our chances play by play, game by game.

BUY A ONE-WAY TICKET

Everything drove me. My team drove me, even as I drove them. My bum shoulder drove me. A passion for the game drove me. Desperation drove me hardest of all. But it's a funny thing about drive. The stronger it is, the more it tends to drive you down paths other than the obvious and the easy, sometimes even against the well-meaning advice of friends and family. My shoulder having failed me, I used that injury to develop all the other skills that would help my team. As a result, I became an All-American high school quarterback who knew how to play and wasn't afraid of center stage. I was always prepared, and therefore full of confidence. As quarterback of a great team—the 1955 victors over almighty Valdosta—I was flooded with scholarship offers in my senior year. I could have gone anywhere, but, in the end, I felt driven to choose my hometown school, the University of Georgia.

Georgia had not courted me. Moreover, during the 1950s it was not fielding great football teams. These two facts alone convinced most of my friends that I was making a big mistake. Even worse, however, was the fact that Georgia already had those two superb quarterbacks, Charley Britt and Tommy Lewis. Yes, my friends did warn me that I would "never get to play." I didn't ignore their warnings; I just didn't buy into them. I never had any doubt that I could and would play, no matter who the other quarterbacks were.

Having led in the win against Valdosta and having been a four-year starter, I knew I was ready for the next step. I was always hungry for the next and tougher challenge. The word for what I felt was *joy.* In deciding to play for Georgia, I never had a doubt that I would start and play and be successful at the University of Georgia, with or without Britt and Lewis.

Naturally, we all like to be praised and told how wonderful we are. The people in our lives who like or love us are usually more than willing to oblige with lavish compliments. Most folks are kind that way, which is a wonderful thing, but not necessarily a good thing. Our automatic response is to lap up all those sugared words, no questions asked. Self-doubt? Most of us do our best to ignore it. The prospect of failure? Better not even *think* about it, let alone talk about it.

I was different. I didn't care how big or fast others were. I knew that both Britt and Lewis had great skills, but, right or wrong, I never doubted that *I* should be the one. I would do anything to succeed: work harder, prepare harder, whatever it took. And I did.

When I later went to play in pro football, I was one of *six* quarterbacks drafted by the Vikings. But I never had a doubt that *I* was going to win the job. If Minnesota had cut me after the fourth week of practice, I had no plan. I had a one-way ticket from Athens to Minneapolis. I was like Hernán Cortés, the conqueror of the Aztecs back in the sixteenth century, who scuttled his ships after landing at Veracruz so that retreat would be impossible. Or like my own good friend and former business partner, the insurance pioneer and founder of LegalShield, Harland Stonecipher. He had grown up dirt poor in Oklahoma and was the first in his family to go to college. He taught school for a while but decided to quit teaching in order to enter the insurance business. He was a fine teacher, and when he told his principal, the man offered to hold open his teaching slot for a year, just in case the insurance venture didn't work out. It was a generous offer that Harland declined. "No thanks. I want you to hire somebody to take my position right now, because I'm afraid if I have a couple of tough days in insurance, having a job to come back to might just tempt me to give up."

Cortés, Stonecipher—I feel the same way. Buy a one-way ticket. Never make it easy to quit.

When I entered Georgia, in 1957, freshmen were ineligible for varsity play, so I played a season with the other first-year players, and we had a great freshman team. We defeated the Clemson, Auburn, and Georgia Tech freshman teams, but the real stunner came when I led the freshmen to a 14-to-7 victory over the *varsity* Bulldogs—one week before they opened their season.

At the time, I knew that Coach Butts planned to "redshirt" me after my freshman year. This meant having me sit out my entire sophomore season, yet still practice with the team. Redshirting had a strategic advantage. It would give me one extra year of (nonplaying) varsity experience plus three full years of eligibility for varsity play, provided that I agreed to graduate after five years rather than the customary four. But strategic or not, I wanted no part of it. Sure, I was just eighteen at the time, but when the coach laid out his redshirt plan, I told him respectfully but firmly that I intended to graduate in four years and that I was ready to play immediately.

After my freshman season, I had no doubt that Coach Butts would see the light and change his mind about redshirting me. But he did not. In his judgment, there was no sense in squandering a year of my eligibility just watching his two established quarterbacks play. To him, redshirting seemed a no-brainer.

But I didn't give up. I *was* going to play. I spent all summer between freshman and sophomore years working out, running up and down the stadium steps, throwing hundreds of balls a day. When August pre-season practice began, I was ready! Work ethic always wins…. Yet, when my first varsity season opened, there I was: the *third-team* quarterback, with the prospect of playing even a single down as a sophomore being precisely equivalent to a snowball's chance in hell. That just made me more determined to find a way to get on the field and help my team. Hell, they needed me!

READ THE SIGNS

Then came September 20, 1958, and the Longhorns' punt, which put us, trailing 7 to 0, in possession of the ball on our 5-yard line. And there was Charley Britt, first-team quarterback, sitting on the bench. At the time, I could not have explained it this way, but what I saw in Britt's sitting on the bench was a sign. I'm not talking about a burning bush, a "sign from heaven." I am talking about seeing one of the signs that are around us all the time and everywhere. They are the myriad details in life and work that show us where to go and what to do—provided we know how to "read" them.

So I saw that sign. I read that sign. And I bolted. Letting my legs carry me onto the field and into the huddle near the end zone, I never looked back.

When I joined the huddle, my teammates gawked at me in total bewilderment.

"What in the hell are *you* doing here?"

"Shut up!" I responded. "We're gonna march this damn ball down the field. Just hang on."

Nobody crowned me quarterback, but I started talking and acting like one, calling plays, making plays, driving our team down the field.

Do you remember *Patton*, that terrific film from 1970? Played to the hilt by George C. Scott, General George S. Patton Jr., the greatest field commander of World War II, quotes one of his heroes, Frederick the Great: *L'audace, l'audace. Toujours l'audace!*—"Audacity, audacity. Always audacity!" What I did in that moment was the height of audacity built on a sense of desperation. I did not wake up that morning planning to simply take the field, but I did wake up desperate and determined to play. I have looked back at that moment often. I have come to understand that people don't change easily. Under normal conditions, change is a hard process, with the odds stacked against it. The greats change. Based now on a lifetime of experience, I've reached the conclusion that the reason the greats change is that they have a sense of desperation and know how to use it to drive change. In 1958, I was eighteen. I'm not telling you that I actually *knew* what desperation was, certainly not as I know it now. But I had an urge. I felt a need. I heard a voice in my head that said, *Go, boy! This is your chance to free yourself.*

As I look back, I realize that if I had not taken the field, Charley Britt would have been quarterback. I would not have played that year, and maybe not have played very much my junior year, either. If I had not played in my sophomore year, I might never have gotten drafted by the NFL. That single moment determined the course of my life. Doing nothing was not an option for me. It was time to take action. I just had to.

Guided by an inner voice? Yes, I was desperate to play. I knew without a doubt that I could make a difference. And I did.

General Patton himself, by the way, would have cheered the advance that resulted. We made a first down followed by another and more, until we reached midfield. Now when we huddled, I had twenty eyeballs looking at me, watching, waiting for me to call the next play. I was their general now. They believed I was their answer.

Focused exclusively on what I could do to enable my team to continue our march, I still avoided looking toward the sidelines. As for Charley Britt, we talked about it all after the game. He told me, "Well, I saw you standing next to Coach Butts, and I just assumed he sent you in!" I responded: "Charley, most of my errors have been errors of assumption." Even back then, I was sharing the lessons I was learning. Assume nothing. Question everything.

So it was focus forward. Advance. First down. Another. Another—in a 90-yard juggernaut to the Texas 5-yard line.

WHEN YOU *CAN* MAKE A DIFFERENCE, *MAKE A DIFFERENCE*

It was third and goal. Now I made it personal, confiding to the guys in the huddle: "Boys, if we don't get this ball in the end zone, I am going to have to take a Greyhound bus back to Athens!" And with that, I took the ball from the center, scrambled, and then passed to our receiver in the end zone, deep in the heart of Texas.

Look, I had acted—well, the polite word is *unconventionally*, but many may think the more accurate term would be *crazy*. As for me, I would just say I had done what was *necessary* in the moment. Sometimes you have to take action, do something *now*. You have to be in the game to make a difference.

CULTIVATE AN ATTITUDE OF DESPERATION

Winning valuable knowledge is a long-term good that pays dividends forever, no matter how much everything else may change. In the short term, though, in the immediate moment, what I did excited my teammates.

I wasn't crazy. I was desperate. I saw my team losing, and I saw an opportunity to make a difference for myself and for my team. I doubt you'll find a professional vocational counselor in the whole wide world willing to tell you that desperation is useful in launching or advancing a career. Too bad. Because what I discovered is that *desperation* is the secret sauce when it comes to doing just about anything worth doing. I make it my business to cultivate desperation. Today, from the time I wake up in the morning to the time I go to bed at night, I create a sense of desperation. It is an energy that drives me and makes me pay attention to "the signs"—those hundreds of details that populate each and every day and that tell you where to point yourself, where to take your team, and what to do next. Just about every successful person I've ever encountered in sports and business alike was desperate and also knew how to make good use of that desperation. The feeling prepared them to be in the moment and to seize the moment—productively. They picked up on every detail. They read the signs, including those that said, *Do something. Do it now. Don't wait.*

GET INTO THE MOMENT AND STAY THERE

Let me just say a little more about "the moment." When I took the field against Texas, I was not consciously thinking beyond the moment. Above all, I was not thinking about winning or losing. In the rest of my football career that followed, in college and in the NFL, I never thought about winning or losing. Not against Texas on September 20, 1958, and never afterward did I stress out reciting a mantra of *We gotta win today!* I never wasted a single distracting thought on it.

To this day, in business, I never worry about winning or losing. In business, as in football, I've always embraced the moment, so that I can focus exclusively on the individual things—the "action items"—I can tick off, one by one, to give us the best chance we have. I focus on solving problems *now*, and if these immediate actions ultimately contribute to a win, great. But all I can directly control is what I can do, right here, right now, concerning the task right before me.

When the moment to act came, I just took it. A decided *bias for action* is key in football and business alike. But please don't get me wrong. In the long run, it is careful planning that provides the edge. As my experience accumulated and grew, I came to understand that one of the most important things I could control was my own level of preparation. I knew I could not control chance or luck or whatever you want to call it. But I could prepare so thoroughly as to make it unlikely that an opponent could surprise me with anything. Armed with this preparation, I could then focus on each play, without so much as a stray thought about the outcome of the play, the quarter, or the day.

A lot of people think there is some special magic in psyching yourself up, convincing yourself that one game—one work day—is more important than another. They sincerely believe that, some mornings, you should tell yourself, *This is the Big Game!* or *This is the Big Day!* Wrong! Every game is important. Every play is important. What you do determines the outcome, so focus on the tasks at hand, one after the other. It is common to pressure ourselves over things we cannot control. But just because it is common doesn't make it helpful.

"YOU ARE NOT BEATEN UNTIL YOU ADMIT IT. HENCE, DON'T."

If I were writing a novel or telling a fairytale, the story would end with the touchdown. But this being football, this being *life*, the game didn't end with that touchdown. We were still behind, 6 to 7. Just when I thought it couldn't get any better, the corner of my eye caught our kicker running onto the field to try for the extra point. It was 1958, the year college football had adopted the two-point option. So I, who had already taken the field without permission, now—also without permission—waved off our kicker!

I heard my team howl, so I howled back: "What did you come here to do? Do you wanna win, or do you wanna tie?"

So I go for the two-point conversion, I find an open receiver in the end zone, and we take the lead, Georgia 8, Texas 7.

As I said, this was football and this was life. It wasn't over, everything can change, everything does, and everything did. Before the game ended, Texas made a comeback with a touchdown, taking the lead from us at 14 to 8. Wouldn't you think Butts would put me in? Well, he did not, and we lost.

I was *pissed*—pissed and puzzled. I just couldn't believe it. And let me assure you, the fact that we ended the game in a loss that would be seen as Charley's loss did *not* make me feel any better. "I told you so" is the most overrated sentence in the English language. No, *we* lost, which made it *my* loss.

But it was also just the first game of the season, not the end of the world. Failure is not final unless, of course, you quit. Losing is part of the game, not a reason to stop playing. I would use the loss as motivating fuel for the rest of the season. As for Coach Butts, having said nothing to me on the sidelines, he said nothing to me on the plane ride back to Athens. Not a word, either of praise or of criticism. He never mentioned it in public, either. In fact, his failure to so much as give a nod to my role in getting the first down—our first in the game—not to mention the 90-yard charge, touchdown, and 2-point conversion that followed, poisoned the Georgia student body and fans against him. Remember, Georgia football was in the dumper throughout most of the 1950s. We were the doormat of the SEC. I had given us hope. So the pressure on Wally Butts built, and he found he had no choice but to start me as quarterback the very next week, against Vanderbilt, or be run out of town.

I was thrilled, of course. He started me, but then he took me out after the first series—just three plays. That is when I got really pissed—not just because he removed *me*, but because it was a stupid move for the *team*. The seeds of my rebellion were planted. They did not sprout until a week later.

Wally Butts was a coach of the old school: loud, pro-fane, a verbally abusive screamer in whose toolbox intim-idation always lay on top. A week after that Vanderbilt game, he lit into Bobby Walden, a Georgia country boy who happened to be one of the greatest punters who ever lived, my roommate, and my good friend. Butts cursed him in front of the whole team. Humiliated him. I saw it. I heard it. It was ugly. I was already mad as hell, but this tirade against Bobby put me over the edge. I was going to do something, and I wasn't going to procrastinate about doing it.

After practice that day, I told my best friend on the team, Pat Dye, who became an All-American and head coach at Auburn, that I was leaving. I told teammates Phil Ashe and Bill "Taterbug" Godfrey that I'd had enough. I told them all I was leaving the University of Georgia. Sud-denly, all three announced they were going with me. Pat's older brother, our team captain, Nat Dye, heard about the looming mass defection and took us to Coach Butts's house for a meeting.

When Coach Butts asked us to explain our problem, the tension built up thick. I anticipated a hell of a blowup. That's when Taterbug, a 190-pound fullback and the

toughest human being I have ever known, a North Carolina country boy who talked like one, the unlikeliest
among us all to speak up, piped in: "We're tired of all that
cussin' you're always doin'."

For me, the tension instantly melted into a fit of laugh-
ter. Why, no one, but no one, not even Wally Butts, could
out-cuss Taterbug Godfrey!

After we left the house, I turned to my guys: "Did he
say anything that made you change your mind?"

"No" was the answer.

"Me neither. Well, I'm going."

The four of us went back to the dorm, and we decided
to meet at Phil Ashe's house in Stone Mountain to make
our plans—all but Taterbug. I reminded him that he was
redshirted, and leaving now would likely mean giving up
his scholarship. It just wasn't worth it. The rest of us
decided that, after spending the night at Phil's, we would
go down to Tallahassee the next morning to sign with
Florida State.

If my life were a movie, what happened next would never
have made it into the script. Any screenwriter would have
crossed it out as pure cornball. But as the saying goes, truth
is sometimes stranger than fiction, and what happened next

really did happen. Morning came, and we ate breakfast at Phil's, fueling up for the drive to Tallahassee.

There was a knock at the door. Phil got up and opened it. It was Quentin Lumpkin, Georgia's freshman football coach and a man we all respected. He was a big guy, gentle and tough, quiet and strong, a man you simply did not mess with. This morning, clearly, he was also a man on a mission. "I talked to Coach Butts," he said, leveling his eyes on me. "I promise you, things will be different if you'll come back. You will play."

Butts had sent us the right guy. We trusted Quentin Lumpkin. If he promised that things would be different, they *would* be different. Because nobody messed with him, not even Wally Butts. We all respected and loved the man precisely because he respected and loved us. He conveyed this to all his freshmen not with sentimental words but through calm, clear, quiet, and invariably wise instruction and counsel. His was a compelling personal presence. Everything he said and did conveyed integrity, transparency, and respect. It made him a leader worth following, and I've never forgotten his example.

Phil and Pat and I looked at each other and nodded. Yes, we are Bulldogs.

Besides: that is what I *wanted* to be! Athens was *my* hometown. My teammates were *my* guys. I believed that, together, we could make Georgia great again, lifting it right out of a decade in the doldrums. Thanks to Coach Lumpkin and his promise, I now had a reason to stay.

What I could not possibly have realized at that moment, however, was that going to the brink of leaving Georgia would be the beginning of a life and career shaped by lessons learned less from winning than from losing, less from success than from failure. I had acted boldly against Texas. *Success!* But then I was out of the game, the Longhorns made a comeback touchdown, and I even failed to win the confidence of my coach. When Butts subsequently berated my teammate, it was (I thought) the last straw. But Coach Lumpkin enabled me to change my mind. Football was about conditioning, smarts, planning, courage, talent, and audacity. I could come up with a hundred more words. Just hearing Quentin Lumpkin's promise, however, convinced me that, most of all, football came down to character.

As our starting quarterback, I went on to lead Georgia to the 1959 SEC Championship, and, on New Year's Day 1960, we won the Orange Bowl against Missouri. I was named MVP. Yes, Wally Butts had kept his promise to Quentin Lumpkin. He played me, and he treated me with respect, but it was not until 1967 that he finally offered actual words of praise. I was attending the College Hall of Fame dinner at the Waldorf-Astoria in New York City. I was playing for the Giants at the time. Coach Butts came up to me, we shook hands, and he said, simply and directly, "You're the best quarterback in football today." I nearly fell on the floor.

PROVE THEM WRONG

Thanks to Quentin Lumpkin's intervention, I was positioned for a highly successful career in college football at the University of Georgia and had great expectations for the 1961 NFL draft, the results of which were announced in December 1960. I had been told that Redskins owner George Preston Marshall was going to draft me for the team I had adored as a boy growing up in Washington, D.C. I was practicing for the Blue-Gray game, and I looked forward to the announcement.

When it came, it was not what I wanted to hear. In the first round, Washington drafted my fellow Gray-squad quarterback Norm Snead. He was a wonderful player from Wake Forest College (now University), and I was sincerely happy for him. But I was also in disbelief.

What about me?

The first round came and went, as did the second. Only in the *third* round was I finally drafted—and not by the Redskins, but by the Minnesota Vikings. Okay, you say, it could have been worse. After all, I hadn't been passed over. I was joining the National Football League! But let me tell you why the news damn near devastated me.

Number one, to be drafted as quarterback in the *third* round pretty much brands you as an also-ran. You may be strong, but not strong enough, and fast, but not fast enough. Cut to the chase: you may be good, but not good enough. Number two, who the hell were the Minnesota Vikings? In 1960, the team did not even exist and would not actually exist until 1961. It was a brand-new franchise and, as with any other NFL expansion team, expectations for a winning season were beyond low.

I was joining the NFL at the bottom rung, and it sure felt like losing. It was a feeling I did not try to ignore or deny. I let it sink in. I owned it—and from the very moment that I took ownership, I decided that I simply would not allow being drafted in the third round by an expansion team to define my career or limit my success. There it was again, that familiar sensation of desperation. The feeling of losing just made me desperate to do whatever I needed to do to win. Whatever else I was *not*, I *was* now an NFL quarterback, and I was determined to prove wrong the Redskins and every other team that did not draft me.

MAKE FAILURE THE FUEL THAT GETS YOU THERE

My desperation never went away. Lucky for me— because it drove me through every season of an eighteen-year NFL career. I was a Pro Bowl selectee nine times. In 1975, the Associated Press named me NFL Offensive Player of the Year, and United Press International named me NFC Player of the Year. Minnesota calls me one of the "50 Greatest Vikings," and I was inducted into the Pro Football Hall of Fame in 1986 and the College Football Hall of Fame a year later.

OWN THE LOSS

Let's admit that not everybody can be successful in the NFL. I was a natural athlete, born that way. I can't take credit for my DNA, but I gladly take credit for working hard to make the most of what I was given, and I gratefully thank everyone, from family, to coaches, to teammates, to fans, who helped me.

Except for the genetic gift, I'm an ordinary guy, not a bolt from the blue or a freak of nature. In fact, my experience in football and in business has taught me that even my attitude toward failure is not unique. Swapping stories with other athletes and entrepreneurs or just reading about them (and I do a whole lot of reading about them) convinces me that almost all truly successful people build their success on a foundation of failure. Before this chapter ends, I'll go on to explain not only why this has always been true, but why today, in a hyper-connected, warp-speed business environment, it is more urgently true than ever before. Later, throughout the rest of this book, I'll tell you about some of my business failures and what they taught me. But before I leave the subject of my football career, let me share the one gridiron defeat I still think about every day. I mean it. *Every* day.

On December 28, 1975, coming off an NFC-best 12-and-2 season, my Vikings were heavily favored against the Dallas Cowboys. But it would end up going another way.

Hardcore fans and football historians remember the game for Roger Staubach's spectacular long pass that gave Dallas the win in the closing seconds of play. An observant Catholic, Staubach commented after the game, "I closed my eyes and said a Hail Mary," and such desperation passes have been known as Hail Marys ever since. Well, Roger is a good friend of mine, and while that pass still rankles me, it was not the thing that got so deeply under my skin.

Turn back the game clock to before the Hail Mary. It was late in the game, and we had the ball at midfield, with a third down and 3 or 4 to go. If we made a first down, the game would be over, the Cowboys would not get the ball back, and Roger's Hail Mary would simply never happen. History is full of such what-if moments. The bottom line on this one? With a first down, the Vikings go on to the NFC Championship game and, quite probably, to the Super Bowl after that. The chances were excellent. We had our best team ever, and, in a dog-eat-dog fight, we were leading Dallas 14 to 10. After a magnificent fourth-quarter drive, we had a third down and short. With five or six minutes left in the game, all we needed was to make a first down on the next play, run out the clock, and claim our victory.

When the hard-pressed Cowboys called a timeout, I stepped over to the sideline to talk tactics with our offensive coordinator, Jerry Burns. He wanted to call a running play, but I wanted to pass. We finally agreed on a rollout to the right and a run for the first down. I was *positive* it was the right call.

In fact, it *was* the best play for that moment. The problem was that we failed to execute. We missed a block. Dallas read the play well, and Charlie Waters, a Cowboys defensive back, busted through our line, blowing the play to bits and, along with it, our "sure-thing" victory in this game as well as an eventual shot at a Super Bowl ring for every one of us.

I could have blamed the failure on our guy who missed the block or on our defense for letting Roger make that Hail Mary. Instead, I took ownership of our failure. As I saw it, the buck both started and stopped with me, the quarterback who had called the play. It was a question of leadership. When you make a decision, you need to acknowledge that things can go wrong and take responsibility when they do. I didn't take ownership to become a martyr or to wallow in misery, but I did use it as motivation to do better next time, and the time after that, and the time after that. It still drives me.

Owning failure means you examine it, rethink it, and figure out how to improve. Our parents tell us things like "Learn from your mistakes." Most of us don't listen—

which is, of course, a mistake! Own a failure, and it is yours to learn from forever. At the very least, you will remember how the failure hurt like hell, and so you'll be motivated never to self-inflict that kind of gut-level pain again. You'll find ways to work harder or to work differently.

Failing and then quitting? The thought has never crossed my mind. As a cadet at West Point, George S. Patton kept a diary. On one page, he wrote: "You are not beaten until you admit it. Hence, don't." I like that. The worst mistake you can make is to think of failure as final. Aside from the fact that both words start with the letter *f,* there is no necessary connection between them. Failure, like success, is a moment in time. Win or lose, there is more on the other side. What you will make of that *more* depends on what you learn from the mere blip of success or failure. No doubt, success feels a lot better. No doubt, failure has a lot more to teach us.

SHARE THE WEALTH: BE GENEROUS WITH FAILURE

So why don't we ever talk about it? I mean *I* just did. But most people—especially leaders, executives, managers, CEOs, administrators, chairpersons—avoid *failure,* both word and subject, as they would day-old sushi or French opera. Failure, it seems, is not a fit topic for polite conversation.

For that matter, neither is *doubt, fear, uncertainty*, or *lack of understanding*. If you are the leader, if you hold any responsibility in an organization, aspire to leadership, or crave promotion to a position of greater responsibility, better not discuss failure or touch on any of those other "negative" states of mind. Just turn around, walk away, ignore them, and they'll all vanish—*poof*! Or so many choose to believe.

Most of us don't talk about failure, because, in our society and within our institutions and organizations, including schools, sports teams, governments, and businesses, failure is considered a shameful thing that merits punishment. You do the math: *Shameful and should be punished + Sounds painful = Better keep my questions, doubts, fears, and failures to myself.*

Keep failure to yourself?

Nothing could be more selfish! Not only to others but, even more, *to yourself*! Nothing has more to teach us than failure, and no motivator is more powerful. As I see it, failure is a gift, and, these days, the business environment is finally catching up with my attitude.

BE BIG ON LEARNING, AND LET EVERYTHING INSPIRE YOU

I'm big on learning. For me, a day that goes by without learning something is a wasted day. So I hedge my bets by starting every day with the *New York Times*, reading it front to back, determined at the very least to know what's happening in the world that day. On Sunday, I add the magazine, which, on November 12, 2014, published "The Innovations Issue." I was probably in the minority of readers who were *not* surprised that one of the issue's lead stories, by Adam Davidson, was titled "Welcome to the Failure Age!"

The piece opens on a warehouse-style store called Weird Stuff, located in the Silicon Valley town of Sunnyvale, California, smack up against Cupertino and Mountain View, home of Apple and Google, respectively. It's the epicenter of innovation. But Weird Stuff is not Apple or Google. It's a kind of secondhand big-box store, twenty-seven thousand square feet in which you can buy the results of innovation that the top-tier retailers and B2B vendors don't offer. These are the products of failure and/ or instant obsolescence: the laptops, desktops, CPUs, disk drives, keyboards, and slick office furniture orphaned when some hopeful start-up went bust; the partitions from cubicles dismantled and dumped when a once-thriving market leader was shoved out of the market by some newcomer offering something brand new.

Like any ancient ruin or modern industrial bone yard, Weird Stuff and its message of failure and impermanence can either depress you or excite your imagination, depending on the point of view you bring to it. Me it excites. As Adam Davidson writes, Weird Stuff reminds us that innovation "is, by necessity, inextricably linked with failure."

In the first place, as Davidson puts it, the "path to any success is lined with disasters." I'm reminded of something I once read about Thomas Edison, our nation's most iconic innovator. In 1878, when he was laboring to find the right material to use as a filament in his electric light, a newspaper reporter asked him how many materials he had already tried and rejected. Edison told him, "About ten thousand." Wide-eyed, the reporter asked how he could possibly endure the heartbreak of such prolonged failure. Edison calmly answered, "I have not failed. I've just found ten thousand ways that won't work." Yes, Edison knew that the path of disaster was the path of knowledge, leading, step by exhausting step, to success.

JOIN THE FAILURE REVOLUTION

But there is more. "Even successful products," Davidson reminds us, "will ultimately fail when a better idea comes along." Edison's once omnipresent incandescent electric light has been elbowed off its godlike throne by energy-efficient fluorescents and even more advanced LEDs.

Unfair? Of course not. We should all of us entrepreneurs be grateful that failure makes so much room for our innovations. In the form of obsolescence, failure clears the way for new products and services, and innovation is nothing less than new opportunity. If you've ever taken your kids or grandkids to see *The Lion King*, you know all about "the Circle of Life." Both innovation and failure are indispensable to what we can call "the Circle of Technology," which continually destroys, creates, destroys, and creates opportunity, markets, and livelihoods.

Like the Circle of Life, the Circle of Technology is hardly a new concept. What Davidson calls the Age of Failure, I prefer to call the Age of Innovation and Failure. It began, literally full steam ahead, in the nineteenth century and exploded big time in the first two-thirds of the twentieth. It was called the Industrial Age, and for every innovation created during it, entire classes of products became obsolete. (Find me a maker of buggy whips or a seller of dial phones.) Yet there was always a heavy cap on the volume of innovation. In the Industrial Age, all truly significant enterprises were capital-intensive. GM, after all, wasn't built in a day or on a dime. The sheer magnitude of money required to start any major enterprise limited the opportunities available to individual entrepreneurs.

Overlapping the Industrial Age, the proliferation of mass media—big newspapers and magazines, movies, and then radio, followed by television—ushered in an Information Age. Information—news, business intelligence, entertainment—vied with industrial products for the leading spot in the global economy. But it still cost a fortune to run a newspaper or build a radio network, make a movie, or start a TV empire. The bar to entry into the Information Economy was almost as high as the bar to entry into the Industrial Economy.

Now, jump to the start of the final third of the twentieth century and the emergence of low-cost "personal" computers. With the desktop, laptop, smartphone, and other personal computing devices and their interconnection via the burgeoning Internet, the door was suddenly thrown open to the individual entrepreneur. In what was now the *Networked* Information Age, the *Networked* Information Economy, just about anybody could start a business. Today, the bar to entry is so low that we currently see 510,000 start-ups each and every month in the United States alone.

Most start-up entrepreneurs fail. That's to be expected. But the fact that most who fail don't try again is completely unnecessary. "You are not beaten until you admit it. Hence, don't." Failure is a point in a life or career, and neither a single failure nor a single success is likely to last long, let alone forever. If the upside of the new Networked Information Economy is tremendous opportunity, the downside is that the calm and comfortable status quo no longer has a safe place to hide. Innovation is now the Golden Ticket, and this means that the demand for any given product or service has a limited shelf life. Today's iPhone is tomorrow's 8-track.

We are in the early days of a Failure Revolution. Join it, and you can accept failure as a step toward success. Deny it or try to hide from it and you risk making failure the end of the line—at least for you. Look, the business world is finally catching up to my personal embrace of failure as an opportunity to learn, to improve, and to win. The question for today's business leaders and entrepreneurs is whether to join the revolution or be kicked to the curb by it. I discovered a long time ago that learning from failure is a *good* business strategy. Today, it is an absolutely *necessary* one. Downright indispensable.

In the next chapter, I'll invite you to walk with me into the Age of Innovation and Failure. I'll show you how the ever-accelerating technology cycle has exponentially increased both the opportunity and the demand for innovation, and how innovation, in turn, has accelerated failure. Even more important, I'll offer real-world strategies, strategies that are designed not to make you *feel* better, but to help you *fail* better—the faster the better. Throughout this book, written for a world of accelerating change, I will also share what I've learned about permanence and the principles of trust, transparency, respect, partnership, and value that are the elements of an enduring culture, which will keep you going through every change in technology or marketing.

Too old for the NFL, I'm still plenty young for an entrepreneur. In fact, I am the perfect fit for this new world built in equal parts of innovation and obsolescence, success and failure, opportunity and obstacle. I warn you, this book is not for everybody. If you are unwilling to admit, own, examine, and embrace failure, read no further. But if you want to advance as a leader, as a creator, as an innovator, then read on.

I wrote this book for entrepreneurs and those who want to become entrepreneurs. More precisely, I wrote it for people who see entrepreneurship not just as a way of business, but as a way of life, as, in fact, the very way *they* want to live *their* lives. If you have no dream of being an entrepreneur, of living the entrepreneurial life, I don't want to sell you the idea. I don't want to convert you to the Gospel of Entrepreneurship. I don't want to change you. But if you are an entrepreneur, or want to become one, or are just thinking about it, you will find in me a partner willing to share his experience, his hard-learned insights, and the insights he's developing every day. My mission in this book is to help *you* be the best entrepreneur *you* can be.

CHAPTER 2

IT'S ALL ABOUT THE WORK

QUARTERBACKS ARE NOT FOOTBALL PLAYERS

WORK FOR THE JOY OF IT

THEY CAN NEVER PAY YOU ENOUGH

MAKE YOURSELF UNCOMFORTABLE

DON'T EVEN TRY TO BALANCE "WORK" AND "LIFE"

COMMIT TO WORK, NOT TO A PRODUCT— TODAY'S IPHONE IS TOMORROW'S 8-TRACK

FAIL FAST SO YOU CAN SUCCEED FASTER

QUARTERBACKS ARE NOT FOOTBALL PLAYERS

Quarterbacks are not football players. Football players block and tackle and hit people, hard. They go mano a mano and nose to nose. While quarterbacks do very few of the basic things football players do, they do more of the basic things that organizational leaders do. They are the CEOs, not the guys on the sales floor and factory floor. They are the field generals, not the grunts and riflemen. Their mission is to study the game, formulate a game plan, and put their players in the best position to succeed. Quarterbacks are the chiefs of the enterprise.

Among the things they must be able to do effectively is read the defense, adapt to changing circumstances, and make good decisions. Typically, they don't have anything like the luxury of time in which to make up their minds, let alone translate their decisions into action. In terms of urgency, decision making is a bar set even higher for a quarterback than it is for, say, the CEO of a supermarket chain. Whereas the supermarket guy can typically think in ninety-day blocks, quarterbacks usually need to evaluate the situation, review options, and call the play right there, on the line of scrimmage. Not surprisingly, they often fail. But, for them, failure is just a situation that requires a new set of fast decisions.

I said in the first chapter that my two high school coaches, Weyman Sellers and Billy Henderson, were so damn demanding—God bless them—that they made college and professional football easy for me, at least by comparison. In much the same way, eight years as a quarterback in high school and college plus eighteen quarterback seasons in the NFL made the transition to creating and leading my own businesses—well, not exactly easy by comparison, but natural and even inevitable. After you have led football teams, especially terrific football teams, it's hard even to consider spending the rest of your working life working for some boss or a faceless sea of shareholders. No matter how much they pay you.

WORK FOR THE JOY OF IT

Now, before I go on, let me correct a word I just used: *transition.*

The truth is that I never actually made a "transition" from *football* to *work*, for the simple reason that I always worked.

At age five, in 1945, I started my first business, offering to haul groceries in my red wagon. I even defined my particular segment of the delivery market: little old ladies, who were grateful for help bringing their purchases from the local Safeway to their doorstep. I earned a nickel and sometimes a dime each trip—and I gave my earnings to my mother, as my contribution to the family's funds. Neither she nor my father asked me to do it, but I was well aware *we* could really use every nickel. Besides, those ladies looked like they could use my help, and helping them felt good. Two years later, when I was seven, I got a paper route, delivering the afternoon news after school every day of the week and then beginning at six o'clock on Saturday and Sunday mornings. That job gave me a little more to throw into the family pot.

Later, when I was in high school, I worked for the mayor of my hometown of Athens, Georgia, Julius Bishop. I was not a fancy political intern or aide. I worked summers on Bishop's chicken farm, a well-known regional institution. Bishop offered ten-hour days and six-day weeks for forty dollars a week. It was my first truly hard job, and I loved it dearly. I found joy in the work, joy that was amplified by the opportunity to create and take pleasure in relationships and by the fact that somebody thought what I had to offer was worth paying for.

Part of most summers, Dad would take us on long road trips—on some as far west as Oklahoma and Colorado—so that he could preach at camp meetings. We had enough money for gas and lodging and for meals at what seemed to me like an endless succession of Howard Johnsons. I always ordered the cheapest thing on the menu, whatever it was. Nobody told me to do it, but I knew we needed to save whatever we could, whenever we could. Like my earnings, it was my contribution to the family, the very first team I knew.

My parents never told me to chip in. But they also accepted my contribution with smiles. The smiles—more like what was behind them—made me feel great about working. It was never really about the money, although that served as a great way to keep score. In the end, I can't tell you for certain whether my joyful need to work was in my DNA—a trait I was literally born with—or the product of my family's financial situation or some combination of the two. All I can say is that I'm glad I never had to find out. Let me tell you why.

In his *David and Goliath: Underdogs, Misfits, and the Art of Battling Giants*, Malcolm Gladwell notes the remarkable fact that "scholars who research happiness suggest that more money stops making people happier at a family income of around seventy-five thousand dollars a year." He explains that if your family's income is $75,000 and your neighbor's is $100,000, the richer family can certainly get "a nicer car and go out to eat slightly more often," but the extra money doesn't make the neighbor happier than you. More important, it doesn't better equip the neighbor "to do the thousands of small and large things that make for being a good parent."

Gladwell is not saying it's good to be poor, and neither am I. I can only imagine how very hard it is to be a parent if there's never enough money to feed, clothe, shelter, and educate your children. Fortunately for me, my parents were able to provide on all four counts, but I also knew that I could contribute monetarily to make *all* of our lives easier and, yes, happier. So I worked.

"It's no great shame to be poor," Tevye the Milkman says in *Fiddler on the Roof.* "But it's no great honor, either." It's no blessing to be poor, but I can tell you that, in my case, it *was* a blessing not to be rich. Gladwell published his book in 2013. Back in 1945, when I hauled groceries in my wagon, $7,700 would buy what $100,000 buys today. Now, maybe I would have worked even if my father had earned the 1945 equivalent of a six-figure income. But Gladwell shows that the odds are against it. He graphs income versus the difficulty of parenting. Picture *wealth* (from poor to rich) on the horizontal axis of the graph and *parenting* (from difficult to easy) on the vertical. From $0 wealth to $75,000, parenting progressively moves from "difficult" toward "easy." But the curve is an arc, not a straight line, and it begins to bend back down toward "difficult" once it crosses the $75,000 threshold. That is, if parenting while really poor is difficult, so is parenting while really rich. Seventy-five thousand dollars in annual income seems to be the sweet spot, producing a level of wealth at which parenting is about as easy as it gets. After that, the curve becomes an inverted U. As Gladwell puts it, "Wealth contains the seeds of its own destruction."

Surprised? Well, why? After all, who of us hasn't heard stories about the "poor little rich girl" (or boy)? Many of us even know, firsthand, children of wealth and privilege who "just can't find themselves," who lack motivation, direction, and ambition, and—nice fat trust fund notwithstanding—who are woefully lacking in happiness. But a lot of us also know kids who received all sorts of material advantages and have made wonderful and inspiring lives for themselves and their families. So, what is the difference between the two? Since external circumstances *required* neither set of kids to work hard, could it be that those in the first category tragically discovered that the need to work was not built in to their DNA, whereas those in the second group joyfully realized the opposite? Wanting for nothing, they nevertheless *needed* to work. And so they did.

Maybe some folks really do have an inborn drive to work and to work joyfully. I believe I do. But I also believe that anyone who wants success can *acquire*—can *learn*—that joyful drive. Moreover, it's never too late to do so. Most of us don't begin our working lives as entrepreneurs. We start out working for some corporation or other organization and only later discover a joyful drive to work for ourselves. These days especially, many people don't find the true joy in work until they "retire" from a thirty-year "day job" and start doing something they really, truly love.

Best of all, they discover the joy of work—a joy that is never all about the money. Don't get me wrong, money *is* important—indispensable, actually—and not just because we all need to make a living. It is deeply satisfying to get well and fairly paid for how you perform and what you do. It is even more profoundly fulfilling if you know that the money you earn provides not only for yourself but for your whole family. The reason it's hard to believe somebody who tells you that money isn't important is that the statement is simply untrue. A Pentecostal preacher, my father worked for a higher power, but he always saw to it that all of us were well fed, clothed, sheltered, and educated here on earth. He knew the importance of money, and he also knew—and from an early age, *I* felt—that money was never the sum total of what it was *all* about. A character in *Death of a Salesman*—the powerful Arthur Miller play that has been made into a number of movies and TV specials over the years—remarks, "No man has enough salary." It's not a statement about minimum wage or earning a hundred grand instead of seventy-five. It's about the fact that money can never be what it's all about. Families with $100,000 a year are no happier than those with $75,000—maybe even a little *less* happy. Better work for the joy of it.

THEY CAN NEVER PAY YOU ENOUGH

No man has enough salary. My salary the first year I played for the Vikings, in 1961, was $12,500 when the median family income in the United States was $5,600 ($44,338.52 in 2014 dollars, according to the Bureau of Labor Statistics). Realistically, I could certainly have supported my small family on today's equivalent of just under $100,000 a year. But I wanted to give them more, and, as I said, I just loved to work. So here's what I mean when I say I never "transitioned" from pro football to business. Throughout eighteen years of an NFL career, I always had an off-season job working for somebody else, a business of my own, or both. In fact, well before I retired from the game in 1978, I began thinking of football not as an end in itself, but as a way for me to finance the start-up of my own businesses.

When I was five, with my red-wagon grocery-delivery service, and seven, with my paper routes, I was a genuine entrepreneur. In high school, however, I worked for Mayor Bishop, on his farm, and in college, between semesters, I sold policies door-to-door for the Franklin Life Insurance Company. I was on scholarship, but I wanted spending money, and I did not want to take any cash away from my parents. I earned enough to buy a car and join the Sigma Alpha Epsilon fraternity. I paid for it all, and it felt good to do so. Besides, I was a business major at Georgia, with a concentration in insurance. What better way to learn more about the insurance industry than by actually selling policies—and getting paid to do so?

Working for others and not for myself probably got me thinking that the best thing in life was to become a top executive in some big corporation. I admit that when I started with the Vikings, I didn't think about building my *own* business. At first, I just looked for an off-season job, and, right after my rookie year, I found one with Wilson Trucking Systems, operating out of Sioux Falls, South Dakota. Wilson shipped through the Dakotas and Minnesota to Chicago. The Interstate Commerce Commission regulated shipping fees, so trucking companies could not compete in terms of price. They had to win customers through service and reliability. By the end of my rookie year as quarterback of an expansion team, I was getting great press and a bit of fame. Wilson paid me $600 a month during January, February, and March to drive hundreds of miles back and forth across these windswept, snow-drifted plains states for the purpose of knocking on the doors of the region's shipping clerks to persuade them to ship with Wilson.

Here I was, a rising pro football star, slogging it out in the bleak midwinter. It was hard, really hard. And I loved it.

Being useful, serving customers, making money for the company that employed me, while bringing in extra cash for my family—what could possibly have been better? Just this: By the time I began my second season with the Minnesota Vikings, I was not only an NFL quarterback, I was a businessman. I soon added to my work for Wilson a modest public speaking career, talking to business, school, and church groups for twenty-five dollars a speech. It thrilled me—the idea of somebody paying me for the words that came out of my mouth. It became the foundation of a public speaking career that eventually earned me $25,000 per speech. And, for years, I gave some seventy-five speeches annually.

After Wilson, I worked the off-seasons for a Minneapolis printer, Holden Press, beating the bushes for contracts and bidding on them. After three winters in the frozen north, however, I decided to warm myself up with off-season employment back in Georgia. I went to work for an Atlanta-based ad agency, Burke Dowling Adams, which put me on two great accounts, one for Delta Air Lines and the other with the State of Georgia's tourism commission. After this, the Coca-Cola Company hired me. I was now a nationally known quarterback, and Coke wanted me to do PR, to make speeches. By this time, however, I wanted more out of an off-season job than a paycheck and an opportunity to work. I also wanted to *learn*. So I told the late, great Don Keough, a Coke executive who would soon become the company's president, that I would make speeches, but that I also wanted to do more. What I wanted, I said, was to go out and learn marketing.

Keough understood instantly. One off-season, he placed me with Coke's ad agency, McCann Erickson, and, in the next off-season, he put me in the Coca-Cola marketing department. In this way, I learned a lot about how business was done by a big company. I got a great education while I was making money. (Later, I was even named to the very first board of directors of Coca-Cola Enterprises, a position I would hold for five years.)

My job with Coca-Cola was my last before starting my own businesses. While I was still playing, I bought into and then bought outright a company called Learning Foundations Inc. It was an extraordinarily rewarding business. With the aid of the latest technology, we developed and implemented tutoring programs in learning centers across the country. Our mission was to help students improve their math and reading skills. By the time I got into Learning Foundations Inc., I was playing for the New York Giants, and Sargent Shriver, a founding force behind the Peace Corps and the founder of the Job Corps, Head Start, and other components of President Lyndon Johnson's War on Poverty, looked me up. He asked if my company could develop "instruction learning" pilot programs in challenged neighborhoods, including New York's Harlem and the disadvantaged parts of Jacksonville, Florida. I told him that I had no doubt we could do it and do it better than anyone else. So we contracted with the government for the programs and made real progress in these two places, dramatically improving reading and math levels.

Our work in Harlem and Jacksonville charged me up. We not only approached the problem intellectually, but at gut level. I hired my teammate the much-loved Giants defensive back Carl "Spider" Lockhart to help drive motivation. A thirteenth-round draft pick in 1965, Spider was a little bitty guy who proved he could knock your ass off, and he was an inspiration to everyone who played with him. The whole experience was incredibly rewarding. If it seems odd that a pro football player, without any experience as an educator, could get charged up as the leader of a company dedicated to education, just know that the greatest passion for a job comes from doing something that helps people. That is why I was so disappointed when our efforts ran afoul of the teachers unions. The issue was this: the unions did not want to be held accountable for the performance of their members. For the union, job security was based on seniority, not merit. If a teacher showed up faithfully and on time for X years, the teacher had a job forever, whether or not the students learned. Running up against the unions, our government-funded programs came to a premature end.

I was so disappointed that the unions were stifling not just us, but the very idea of an educational meritocracy. In so doing, they were cheating students, especially at-risk students, out of a better future. What kept me going was the knowledge that we hadn't failed. I was, in fact, encouraged and inspired by the results we achieved.

In 1970, Don Rumsfeld, who was then director of the Office of Economic Opportunity (OEO) for President Nixon (and who would eventually become White House chief of staff and, twice, secretary of defense), hired us to create and run a minority-oriented jobs program intended to reinvigorate the ailing textile mills of the South. Working the programs in Harlem and Jacksonville had taught me a lot about education, and I was confident I could now learn what I needed to know about the textile industry and its workers. I also knew that I could not do this alone. So I partnered with a most remarkable man: Dr. Aubrey Daniels, a clinical psychologist who in 1970 was working in an Atlanta mental hospital. He was developing advanced methods of training and motivation based on the work of behavioral psychology pioneer B. F. Skinner. Daniels created what he called "performance management"—today a cornerstone in employee development—and, together, we implemented it in our work for the OEO.

Our mission was to create an environment in which workers could learn and succeed. For this to happen, we had to train their supervisors—their "coaches"—most of whom had no education beyond high school and all of whom were set in their ways. We had to train them to be better coaches to their workers. The southern textile mills were plagued by low productivity and inefficiency due to poor employee performance, spotty attendance, and a disastrous rate of turnover, often in excess of 100 percent. As a result, the mills were under threat from foreign competition, and if they were shuttered, thousands of workers—many of them poor blacks—would have been out of work. We were tasked with reversing all the negative trends, converting inefficiency into efficiency, elevating employee performance, improving attendance, and putting the brakes on turnover.

I traveled to Fort Mills, South Carolina, home of Springs Industries, and introduced myself to Bill Close, president of the company, which operated forty or fifty mills in the state. I talked to him about the federal initiative and told him I believed we could help his plants and his company. He agreed to give us a chance, and Aubrey Daniels and I took our teams into the plants, putting trained behavioral scientists in each plant. We focused on changing the mindset of the supervisors. As I saw it, this meant getting down on the plant floor so that we could understand the issues from their point of view. We did it, and we got tremendous results, reducing turnover, for example, from 110 percent to 50 percent, increasing revenue for the company, and making the lives of the workers better, more productive, and a lot more secure. Dr. Daniels and I realized that we had the start of a groundbreaking industrial management training company.

But we soon ran into an apparently insoluble problem. While the management of Springs Industries was willing to give a government-funded program a try, we met with stout resistance as we attempted to expand beyond this company. Most textile moguls were dead set against taking federal funds for anything. Instead of giving up and assuming that, without federal funding, we were dead in the water, I did what I learned to do working for Wilson Trucking Systems. I knocked on doors, beginning with Cannon Mills, the largest towel maker in the world. The personnel director there was Asbury ("Bury") Hudson, a six-foot-five former University of South Carolina basketball player. We hit it off right away (my middle name is Asbury!), and I proposed that Cannon Mills, not the government, fund a six-month program for us to teach the principles of performance management at their plant in Kannapolis, North Carolina. Bury agreed. Not one to risk momentum on lawyers and bean counters, I wrote out a contract over lunch, on a napkin: $9,500 a month for six months. By the end of six months, we decreased turnover and absenteeism and greatly improved productivity. From this seed, we went to hundreds of textile plants throughout the South: from Cannon Mills to Burlington Industries, Deering Milliken (later Milliken & Co.), Dan River, and others.

Daniels and I created a new company, Behavioral Systems Inc., and our methods of performance management were so compelling that we soon expanded from the South and the textile industry to industries nationwide. We flourished, rapidly evolving from the government-funded offshoot of a tutoring company into something entirely private sector, a company that brought to often-struggling industries and hard-pressed workers the benefits of a new science. Best of all, even as it enhanced lives in ways hard to describe, the value we delivered could be measured very clearly in upward-moving revenue numbers.

No, I was not a professional psychologist—although every good quarterback is at least partly an amateur psychologist. I had no formal training in human resources or industrial management. But I worked with the best in the field, I learned from him, and I listened to our clients. I was passionate about bringing value, solving problems, and delivering results. Damn, it was fun! Ultimately, my interests would lead me into other, more tech-oriented directions, but Aubrey Daniels took what we had begun and turned it into a major and enduring practice. By my reckoning, our company, Behavioral Systems Inc., spawned a dozen, perhaps fifteen, similar companies founded by the behavioral scientists who worked for us. I felt—I feel—I've made a mark on the American workplace.

MAKE YOURSELF UNCOMFORTABLE

Looking in from the outside, it undoubtedly seems strange that I, a pro quarterback, should be getting into a tutoring business and then a management training business. I'll admit it was not business as usual. Well, "business as usual" is not the stuff of innovation, is it? Innovation is business *unusual*. It's about actually *doing stuff* so that you can learn from the doing. My whole life had been—and still is—about learning and teaching. I learned everything I could about football, and I used football to finance my practical education in business. As a quarterback, I was always a teacher as well as a student. Jerry Burns, my coach at the Vikings, once even described me as his "co-coach." And that is what a good, conscientious quarterback is. So getting into a teaching company was not such a random turn, even viewed from the outside. Viewed from the *inside*, it was, in fact, the perfectly natural product of my drive to create businesses that help people, solve problems, deliver value, and produce measurable benefits. Collectively, these criteria have always been the yardstick by which I judge any business, including my own.

I do have to tell you, however, that my life and career took another turn just before I retired from professional football, and this one *does* seem rather random, even to me. Right after we lost the Super Bowl to the Oakland Raiders on January 9, 1977, I received word that *Saturday Night Live* wanted me to guest-host the show. *SNL* had debuted in 1975 and was a hit right away, but I was one of very few people who had never heard of the show. (Okay. Back in the 1960s, I was so focused on my football career, I didn't know who the Rolling Stones were—a fact my wife laughs about to this day.) I soon learned, however, that *SNL* drew a large and growing young audience. The prospect of appearing on this *live* show made me very uncomfortable. But the more uncomfortable it made me, the more I decided I wanted to accept the challenge. Besides, I would be the very first professional athlete to host *Saturday Night Live*.

As I see it now—and as I saw it back then—you learn the most about career, life, business, and yourself by taking every opportunity to move outside of your comfort zone. By definition, the comfortable and the familiar have nothing new to teach you. The most successful people in life and business are innovators. By definition, innovators need to be uncomfortable. They seek unfamiliar places, situations, and people. Familiarity, after all, cannot be counted on to provoke new thinking. And, hell, I thought it would be fun. Besides, just as I was using football money to finance my businesses, I figured I could use whatever celebrity I had to pave the way for more business opportunities. Whatever else my football career was, it was the capital of my personal brand. It couldn't hurt to add to that capital.

So, on January 29, 1977, I appeared as a guest host on *Saturday Night Live*. That the opportunity came to me so quickly was a blessing. I didn't have time to develop stage fright or to overanalyze the task at hand.

As a football player, I knew I couldn't control an opposing team. I could only control my own level of preparation, practice, and execution. But I *knew* how to play football; I knew nothing about TV. I could not act, I could not sing, I could not tell jokes. Still, I approached the big-time network TV show the way I approached football—by preparing myself as best I could. I learned my lines, I asked questions, and I studied how *SNL* performers like Bill Murray, John Belushi, Dan Aykroyd, and Gilda Radner rehearsed their skits. By treating the cast and crew as teammates in a big football game, I put myself at ease—and I discovered I was damn good at reading a teleprompter!

I also discovered that *I* had something to teach. I costarred in the opening skit with John Belushi, a high school football jock and a big fan. My writer was none other than Al Franken, a great comic who, these days, is a U.S. senator from Minnesota and a good friend. Belushi and Franken asked *me* to tell *them* what really goes on in a professional football locker room before a game. So I did. "We have a prayer," I explained. "Bud Grant, our coach, usually taps the most religious guy on the team to make a suitable address to God Almighty. We all bow our heads, and the prayer goes something like, 'Dear Lord, we ask that you protect everyone in the game, see that there are no injuries and that everybody plays fair and plays well ...' The main thing is that the prayer never includes *anything* about winning. It's all nice and vanilla."

I paused after this. "Then, as soon as the prayer is over, we all jump up and holler like madmen, 'Let's go out and kill those sons of bitches!'"

And *that* was my contribution to a live network TV show. What I took away from that experience was something General George S. Patton told his junior staff officers: "We can all learn from each other." It's a lesson I've carried into every business I've led since. I don't have all the answers, but I do have a lot to teach my employees and partners. And I also have a lot to learn from them. Business would be awfully dull if this weren't true.

Anyway, after Thursday's rehearsal, I thought I was home free and all set for Saturday night. First, however, came a run-through in front of a studio audience. As a result of this, the whole opening was changed! No one could have blamed me if I panicked at this point, but I did no such thing. Instead, I again fell back on what I had learned from football: control what you can, and don't worry about the rest.

"Boys, this is just like a game," I told Belushi and Murray. "Nothing's gonna intimidate me. They're gonna put something up on that teleprompter, and we'll just go from there."

I don't mind telling you that I knocked the cover off the ball. (NBC recently featured my appearance in an *SNL* anniversary "best of" compilation!) After *SNL*, I got some commercial endorsements and speaking gigs—lots of those: about seventy-five a year, at first at $25,000 a speech and sometimes $50,000. With money like that, I took just about any engagement—at least at first. On one occasion, I was asked to talk about the secrets of pro football training—conditioning, nutrition, and so on. Now, you would think that would be an easy subject for me. Trouble was that in the 1970s, "training" was almost nonexistent. We practiced, of course, but no one prescribed special diets or assigned personal trainers to customize some secret workout regime. The guy we *called* a "trainer" mostly did just one thing. He taped our ankles. Well, I gave the speech anyway, talking for twenty or twenty-five minutes about "training," but I have no idea what I said. I do remember that I left the podium smiling but feeling terrible because I had delivered nothing of value. I promised myself that from then on, I would speak only on subjects of my own choosing, subjects about which I knew I had something of genuine value to say. And I've kept my promise.

By my retirement from professional football in 1978, the year after I hosted *Saturday Night Live*, I already had my own businesses going. What I did not have any longer, of course, was football to finance my start-ups. So when ABC asked me to join *Monday Night Football*, I signed up as a color commentator beginning in 1979. After all, I was already a veteran of *SNL*, and this was a lot easier. I don't remember what they paid me, but they paid me a lot of money—I think about $25,000 per show, certainly enough to bankroll some of my own start-up ventures.

The next year, 1980, while I was still doing *Monday Night Football* and three years after I first appeared on *SNL*, Alan Landsburg, a Hollywood producer, called me. He was going to do a show called *That's Incredible!* It was to be an early entry in the reality show genre, and it showcased everything from gee-whiz breakthroughs in science and technology to guys who juggled knives and caught bullets between their teeth. One show even featured the putting of a five-year-old golfer, name of Eldrick, who, two years *earlier,* had shot a 48 over nine holes at Cypress Navy and had just appeared in *Golf Digest.* When he grew up, he became better known as Tiger Woods.

Now, I wasn't being asked to do anything with knives or firearms, and I wouldn't have to play golf with a five-year-old, but the show did need a team of hosts. They'd done a pilot with singer-actor John Davidson, actress Cathy Lee Crosby, and Jim Palmer, pitcher for the Baltimore Orioles. For some reason, Palmer didn't quite gel as part of the trio. Landsburg saw me on *Saturday Night Live* and asked me to come to LA. He didn't even want to audition me. "We'd like you to do it," he said, and from 1980 to 1984, we shot twenty original shows a year in addition to ten compilations. It was long hours, since we shot several shows a day, and much of the time was in setup. Instead of holing up in my trailer until I was needed onstage, however, I invested my downtime observing everybody and asking questions. I'm not talking about just my cohosts, but also the grips, gaffers, prop people, directors, assistants, you name it. I figured it was an opportunity to learn as much as I could about television production while getting paid $25,000 a show, with thirty episodes a year. Far more important, I built relationships and trust at all levels of the television community, and made some very good friends, especially John Davidson, who has been a pal ever since. Relationships are key to creating a successful and enduring business. They are the fabric of its culture and therefore trump everything. You have a far better chance of surviving a flawed business strategy than of surviving flawed business relationships.

I was now making more money as a media "personality" than I ever had playing football. And when I left the NFL, I was making $275,000 a year. Those were 1978 dollars, which made me the highest-paid professional football player at that time. I'd like to tell you that I'm not bragging, but, of course, I *am* bragging. Anybody looking at my career from the outside would conclude that I had leveraged my eighteen-year run in professional football to build a lucrative career in TV, but actually it was just another means to finance my businesses. Business—not football and certainly not TV—was the constant, and before we're done with this chapter, I'll tell you why I was so determined to bootstrap my own ventures rather than borrow money to start them.

My businesses—hands-on, fingers-in-the-soil businesses—were and are my passion. People will tell you they are *passionate* about their career. Offer them a whole bunch of money, however, and see what happens to their passion. It's a test, really. Will several million pretty easy dollars per year persuade you to change course from entrepreneur to "media personality"? Not me. In fact, I left *Monday Night Football* in 1982 and *That's Incredible!* two years after that.

Working on a farm, selling life insurance door-to-door, driving all over South Dakota and Minnesota in midwinter—I actually loved all that. I also loved working with Howard Cosell, Don Meredith, and Frank Gifford, but three years talking about what *other* football players were doing—"Nice catch!" "Great pass!"—was three years too many. I wanted to be on the field and in the action. I didn't want to talk about it. Being a color commentator on *Monday Night Football* was the only job that ever bored me. As for *That's Incredible!*, I was not an actor, and I was not an entertainer. I could read a teleprompter, and I certainly had a "personality," but these were not assets that reached into my heart and soul. Sure, the money was great, but unlike Learning Foundations Inc. or Behavioral Systems Inc. or the businesses I operate today, it didn't help people or make the world a better place, and I wanted to do something more.

DON'T EVEN TRY TO BALANCE "WORK" AND "LIFE"

That brings me to one of the saddest, most corrosive buzz-phrases of our time: *the work/life balance.* To me, that phrase seems to come down to this: when you're working, you're supposed to feel guilty that you're taking time away from your "life," by which most people mean their family; but when you're spending time with your family or in some leisure activity, you're supposed to feel guilty about not working and advancing your career. Work-life *balance*? According to a 2014 Harvard Business

School survey of nearly four thousand C-suite executives, most women plead guilty to neglecting career or family. Most men simply slink out of the courtroom.

"When you are paid well," a successful woman executive told a survey interviewer, "you can get all the [practical domestic] help you need. What is the most difficult thing, though—what I see my women friends leave their careers for—is the real emotional guilt of not spending enough time with their children. The guilt of missing out." A successful male executive, in contrast, boasted to interviewers that the "10 minutes I give my kids at night is one million times greater than spending that 10 minutes at work." Male executives readily confess that they "don't prioritize their families," but they're just not bothered much about it. Instead, they "praise their spouses for taking over the homefront entirely."

Two things really bother me about the Harvard survey. First, while women accounted for 46.9 percent of the U.S. labor force in 2012 and held a whopping 51.5 percent of management, professional, and related positions, both men and women tend to see the work/life balance as a woman's problem. Second, while women cop a plea and men flatly refuse to stand trial, both appear to be more concerned about being judged guilty—or about *feeling* guilty—than they care about actually shortchanging either family or career. So, it isn't really that work and life are out of balance. It's the majority's *view* of work and life that is way out of whack.

Let's recognize right now that the work/life balance is less about divvying up hours between career and family than it is about feeling guilty no matter how we apportion our time. The "crime" is neither neglect of family nor compromising your career. The crime is *guilt* itself. And who needs *that*?

Feeling guilty poisons both career and family. You cannot divide yourself mathematically between the two. Instead, get into the moment every moment. When you are working, devote 100 percent to the job at hand. When you are with your family, *they* get 100 percent from you. As far as time goes, understand that being an entrepreneur *takes* plenty of effort and time, but it typically *gives* you more control over your time. This is one of the most attractive things about starting your own business. Putting yourself at the mercy of a schedule dictated by a boss or a board or a quarterly earnings target relinquishes control. Working for yourself gives you control of all of your time, but it's up to you to deliver 100 percent, 100 percent of the time, in an effort to be the greatest entrepreneur, the greatest spouse, the greatest parent, the greatest grandparent—the greatest at whatever means the most in your world.

Give yourself a test. Are you ever too busy to return a phone call from a family member, an employee, a customer, a vendor? Do you delay answering e-mails as long as you possibly can or maybe forever? Do you habitually put off requests for face-to-face meetings? If you answer *yes* to any of these questions, you are declaring to the world that you have no time for the fundamentals of humanity. What should you do? Fix it. Now.

But let's not make the mistake of focusing exclusively on time. The activities we call *work* and those we call *family* both take place in the dimension of time—of course. But they are not *about* time. If you do nothing more than "spend time" at work or "spend time" with your family, you are putting yourself in a sad and soul-killing situation. Intolerable.

Time with career and time with family are best *invested* in things that bring profound value to both career and family. That is why it is so important to identify your passion. Know what you value and then imbue your whole life—career and family, family and career—with those values. Don't sell out one for the other.

What are you doing right now? If you find yourself worrying over work-related guilt and family-related guilt, stop squandering valuable time on guilt and instead invest some time in reflecting on your priorities. Discovering your passion, determining what nourishes rather than drains you—what renews you rather than uses you up—will enable you to define your values. Once you have done this, you can bring those values to career and family alike. You will be delighted to find that applying values to the place where career meets family makes the joint utterly seamless. The division between work and life will disappear, and with the disappearance, both work and life will become—simply—*living*.

I left the "easy money" of *Monday Night Football* when I realized that the job actually cost me too much. Feeling bored was a sign. "Reading the signs" was something I learned from the great Bud Grant, the Vikings' inimitable coach. One day, he announced during a team meeting that players were trampling over a bare patch of turf the groundskeepers had just seeded.

"There's a sign there that says *Keep off the grass*," Grant scolded us, "so, keep off the grass."

It struck me as odd that our head coach would go out of his way to make a big deal about a little patch of grass. My puzzlement came to an end the very next day, when Bud pulled me aside just before practice. He asked me to meet him in his second-floor office. There I found him, back to the door, gazing out the window. He was watching my teammates walk from the meeting hall to the practice field.

He motioned to me, and I stood next to him at the window.

What we both saw is that most of the players conscientiously walked around the area marked by the *Keep off the grass* sign. A few, however, strolled straight across it.

"The guys who went ahead and walked on the grass seed aren't being defiant," Bud remarked to me. "They didn't see the sign. They didn't see the sign, either because they weren't paying attention to me yesterday, or they weren't paying attention as they walked today. In either case, those are the players who will make dumb mistakes that will cost us the game. They don't pay attention to the signs around them."

I was amazed by the observation, which revealed just how detail-oriented a great coach is. I was even more amazed when it became clear that Bud Grant was right on the money. Throughout the season, I kept an eye on those players who had ignored the *Keep off the grass* sign—at least those who managed to stay on the team. They were, for a fact, the players who made the most mistakes and the costliest mistakes. Bud Grant was right. These men were not alert to what was going on around them. They did not see, read, or heed the signs.

Being bored by *Monday Night Football* was a sign I was not about to ignore. It told me that I was not living my values. I wanted, I needed, to be *in* the arena, making things happen, not just watching them. So I quit to devote myself to businesses that I loved, doing what allowed me to live my values wherever I was—at home or at the office, with my family or with a client. When you feel driven by purpose, time ceases to be a problem. It actually seems to expand, or stop, or simply recede into the background. This is because you are living in the moment every moment, on the job or with your family or by yourself, doing and experiencing genuine meaning and real value, living a purpose-driven life.

COMMIT TO WORK, NOT TO A PRODUCT— TODAY'S IPHONE IS TOMORROW'S 8-TRACK

Like the quarterback, the entrepreneur works in a cycle of success-failure-success. In business, this cycle parallels the innovate-fail-innovate rhythm found throughout much of today's business environment, especially among enterprises introducing new products and services or new approaches to established products and services. The upside of our new Networked Information Economy is tremendous opportunity. That's why we currently see 510,000 U.S. start-ups a month.

The downside? The status quo no longer offers a safe place to hide. Innovation is now the Golden Ticket, and this means that the demand for any given product or service doesn't last for long. Today's iPhone is tomorrow's 8-track. A commitment to innovation means a commitment to trying, failing, learning, and trying again. Your commitment should not be to *the product*, it should be to *the work*—work is *the* permanent feature of successful entrepreneurship; it is how you innovate, navigate, or adapt to inevitable change

I'll give you an example. One day, back in the early 1980s, I was standing in line at an airline ticket counter, checking in for an Atlanta-bound flight after a three-week Hawaiian vacation.

Technically, I was still on vacation. *Actually*, I was working. I couldn't turn it off, even if I wanted to. And I never want to. Waiting in line, I picked up on something nobody, including me, usually gave any thought to—at least not back in the day of the paper airline ticket, years before the era of the e-ticket. People at the counter, walking toward the gate, sitting and waiting—everyone—carried an airline ticket slipped into an airline-issued ticket jacket.

Okay, so it wasn't exactly the same as the falling apple knocking the idea of gravity into the head of Sir Isaac Newton. But what was to others a reality too mundane to think about was to me a sign.

It hit me that a lot of air travelers are among the more affluent consumers. It also struck me that commercial air travel is essentially boring. Seated on a long flight, drink at the ready, people read whatever comes to hand. It could be a book, a magazine, or a ticket jacket. What could you print on a ticket jacket for people to read?

Visions of ticket jackets followed me all the way to Atlanta and even into my bed that night. At some point before the onset of unconsciousness, it occurred to me that those ticket jackets, carried by millions of bored airline passengers with money to spend, were a resource begging to be exploited. Here was a stiff paper envelope that you wouldn't throw away until your trip was finished. Paper. Paper was made to be printed on. That night it dawned on me. These ticket jackets, which the airlines regarded as strictly utilitarian, were miniature billboards or advertising brochures waiting to happen.

In the bright light of an Atlanta morning, I realized that my idea came with at least three problems. Number one, I wasn't in the advertising business. Number two, I wasn't in the airline business. Number three, I wasn't in the printing business. But, fortunately, I also realized I *was* in the problem-solving business, and here were *three* to solve. Business was booming!

At the time, I was a commercial spokesman for Delta Air Lines. The first thing I did was call a friend at Delta. I did what I always do, which is to ask him a lot of questions, rather than give a lot of answers. Mainly, I wanted to know how many ticket jackets Delta printed and distributed monthly and annually. The numbers were even bigger than I had imagined. Repeating the number back to him, I asked him what would happen if I offered to print all those ticket jackets for Delta for free. Would the airline be interested? Of course they would.

I called a few more airlines, and pretty soon I knew something about the airline ticket-jacket business. Next, it seemed to me, I had to reach out to a printer, since I had neither the desire nor the capital to start my own printing company. I started calling local printers. Unfortunately, none had the capacity to print the quantities I needed. So I asked whether they knew of a printer anywhere in the country that could handle the job. The name of a Chicago firm kept coming up. I called them and set up a meeting with the company's president. His name was Tony Jacobs, and I told him that I wanted to discuss a long-term job for which his company was one of very few that had the capacity. That got the necessary attention, and I flew out.

Having a name many people recognized helped open doors, but I've never closed a deal without bringing real value to the table. Most professional athletes fail in business because they have no idea how to bring value to a business. You can be the greatest sports hero in the world, but if you walk into a business offering nothing more than your name, it will be a very short and unproductive meeting.

When I sat down with Tony Jacobs, I knew that what was on *his* mind was how *I* could bring additional value to *his* business. I therefore presented a simple proposition, telling him that if he could print fourteen million ticket jackets a month, I would pay him for the printing and give him a 50 percent ownership stake in the business. Do you want great partners? Make certain that you put them in a position to make money.

From his point of view, it was a very attractive deal. He owned a lot of big, hungry, costly printing presses that demanded to be fed. I was proposing to feed them. As for me, I owned nothing but an idea. To both of us, a 50/50 split seemed more than fair.

With a super-high-capacity printer on tap, it was time to meet with more airlines. Now I was armed with more than an idea. I had a printer—and not just any printer, but one with massive capacity. I also had the answer to a problem airlines didn't realize they had: the cost of printing millions of ticket jackets. I told the airlines that I could furnish all the ticket jackets they would ever need, for free. With just two exceptions—Braniff and Eastern—every airline I approached signed up, not to make me money, but to add value to their own companies.

I had approached the printer with nothing more than an idea. I approached the airlines with an idea and a printer. Tony Jacobs assured me that his eleven-person sales staff would sell out the advertising space in nothing flat. That was a good thing. It was nearly June, and we had a September deadline for a January launch. Imagine my—well, let's call it "consternation," when, by late June I discovered that not one of Tony's eleven salespeople had managed to sell a single page of advertising.

At the time, I was a single father. I had committed to spend the entire month of August with my kids. That commitment was sacrosanct. I was currently doing *That's Incredible!*, and I had a number of other companies to operate. All I had, then, was three weeks in July to make all the sales: twelve pages of advertising. I called on a friend, Marvin Bluestein, who knew no more about advertising than I did, but who was sharp (even if he *was* a Georgia Tech grad), had the personality of the aspiring actor that he was, and was also one of the greatest small-business people I had ever met. After explaining the business to him, I ended with a simple statement of our mission: "Marvin, we're going to New York, you and me, and we're gonna sell this sucker out."

The two of us set up shop in Manhattan's Waldorf-Astoria Hotel the weekend after the Fourth of July and went to work on our high-end prospects. For the next three weeks in the capital of advertising and corporate America, Marv—at five foot two, a kind of gray-haired Danny DeVito—and I made for a strikingly odd couple in the C-suites of AT&T, Exxon, General Motors, Eastman Kodak, MasterCard, and the like. Whatever else happened, I knew we would make an impression. More important, I was confident that we would make the sales—and we did. Before the end of the month, we did "sell this sucker out," each page going for $100,000 per month for a twelve-month commitment. That put our take at $1.2 million times twelve. It was a lot of money. The fact that it was a lot of money produced by hard work made it even better.

The skin-of-our-teeth launch of Ticket Marketing Inc. was, in fact, a spectacular success, and I congratulated myself on having one of the Great Ideas of the Century.

Even before a year had passed, however, I saw, read, and heeded the signs that my beloved brainchild was not destined to become a sustainable big business. First, we had no measuring tool to evaluate the impact of the advertising on the revenue of our subscribers. Second, the airlines didn't take the product seriously. They had no incentive to do so. What they were getting was free ticket jackets. That's all. And if, at the end of the year, they had jackets left over, they kept using them. So the current ads were often inadequately distributed. Sure, Ticket Marketing Inc. made money—just not nearly as much as I thought it would. Everybody got paid, but the return on the advertising did not bowl over our $100,000-a-month clients.

Bad news doesn't get better with age. As soon as I had figured out the signs, I called Tony Jacobs to tell him that the company was not big enough to make sense to me and that I could either shut it down or give it all to him. I offered Tony my 50 percent at no cost and with my blessing. So he took over the company, ran with it for a while, and then eventually shut it down, having lost nothing and, in fact, having made a modest return.

Ticket Marketing Inc. failed to meet my hopes and expectations, but it still made some money, and its ultimate failure did not make *me* a failure. On the contrary, getting out of the business was a successful business decision, helping me to move on to other, bigger and better things. "Failures" like this are a fact of business life—but knowing *when* to shut something down—a project, a product, a business—is not a failure, it is what successful enterprises and their leaders do.

FAIL FAST SO YOU CAN SUCCEED FASTER

Ticket Marketing Inc. was not the first company I started. My first *major* venture was born in 1968, while I was playing for the New York Giants. Fast food was a growth market with many competing chains trying to catch up to McDonald's. A friend of mine pitched me the idea of creating a kind of fast-food smorgasbord where you could get anything you wanted: a burger, a pizza, a hot dog, fried chicken. It was meant to be like every fast-food place rolled into one. It sounded like a great idea, and maybe it even was.

Partnering with my friend, who also happened to be my lawyer, I quickly closed on a promising location on Atlanta's Piedmont Road and opened up a restaurant we called Scrambler's Village.

My partner and I were confident that *this* Scrambler's Village would be the first of many—a lucrative national franchise in the mold of McDonald's. At the age of twenty-six, I had a terrific bias for action. I still do, in fact, and I think it's essential to an entrepreneur. You never really know if an idea will work until you *do something*. You don't learn until you get stuff done. If you are excited by an idea, act on it. An advantage small businesses have over bureaucracies is they can act now. But while passion and a bias for action are *essential* to the entrepreneur, they alone are not sufficient to drive a sustainable business.

My lawyer and I acted—not by taking a step from which we could, if necessary, step back, but by jumping in with both feet. We bought the real estate. We built the restaurant. We spent a load of money. But we didn't study the market—hell, we didn't even ask the most basic questions, like what really should be on the menu and, equally important, what should *not*. It was the *Field of Dreams* approach: *Build it and they will come.* Trouble is, "they" never did. Our menu was untested, our market was unknown, and we were unknown within the market. Planning, preparing, recruiting, and training—all these take time, and we didn't give it any. Fast food? Scrambler's Village proved to be a fast failure. It closed six months after opening.

Now, let me correct myself. I've been using the plural pronoun *we*. In fact, "we" didn't set out to create Scrambler's Village. I made the mistake of giving my lawyer my money and my nationally known nickname ("The Mad Scrambler," "Scrambling Fran"), and then I stood back, waiting for the cash to flow in. I started Scrambler's Village because I wanted a business, and my lawyer's idea sounded like a good one. But I had no connection to the restaurant business, and, in fact, if someone had handed me a McDonald's franchise complete with experienced cooks and counter people, I still would have failed because I had no idea how to run a restaurant.

The thing is, my lawyer—to whom I handed over the reins—knew nothing more about fast food (or slow food, for that matter) than I did. Lawyers are bad businesspeople because they're not businesspeople, they're lawyers. Lawyers are also bad neurosurgeons, they're terrible dentists, and they aren't much good at architecture either. My lawyer was a terrific lawyer, but he was not a businessperson, or a chef, or a restaurateur. Yet I handed him my money, my nickname, and my new business. To outsource this way is to surrender before the battle begins.

To make matters worse, the money I gave him was money I borrowed.

Yes, it is a good idea to *do something.* But you also have to be patient enough to realistically assess the need for your product or service and then to make sure that what you roll out is actually ready to roll out—not to mention worthy of being rolled out. And the launch is just the beginning. You, yourself, personally need to ride herd on the operation, especially during the first several days, weeks, and months. You may need all the help you can get—from people who have hands-on expertise in *your* business, not theirs—but your full presence is absolutely mandatory. Your hands have to be in the soil. In the beginning especially, hundreds, maybe thousands, of revisions, adjustments, and tweaks will be needed once you see how things are working (or not) and get feedback (good, bad, and ugly). This extended rollout period is when you can learn the most you will probably ever learn about your business. It is fatal to miss out on it. So, eyes open, ears open, mind open, and mouth shut—except to ask questions and thank people for their criticism, the harsher the better.

There's no question that Scrambler's Village was a financial failure, but, in every other way, it was a success. First, I knew enough to shut it down before it brought me down. Second, I learned from it. I learned the crucial importance of knowing what you know and what you do not know. I learned that it is essential to hire the expert help you need while keeping your own hands firmly on the business. I made it a personal rule never again to turn over any business of mine to others—not to a lawyer and fraternity brother, not to a bank or a venture capitalist, and not to a rich uncle either. A lawyer knows the law, a banker or a venture capitalist knows money, and your rich uncle might be a swell guy, but none of that relates to the day-to-day running of *your* business. After Scrambler's Village, I decided that I would figure out ways to boot-strap any future venture without going outside to borrow cash. And later, when I could compare my Scrambler's Village experience with my experience with Ticket Marketing Inc., I realized I had learned the advantage of developing a business one small step at a time.

Scrambler's Village was a painful disappointment. But it did give me one of the great gifts of failure. From the experience, I learned perhaps the only unbreakable rule of entrepreneurship: *the faster we fail, the faster we succeed.*

Lose money I did, but—and this is more important—I lost very little time and, in the end, none of my enthusiasm. Surviving the venture, learning from it, and remaining eager to start new things made me a success, even with scrambled egg on my face. By the time I retired from professional football ten years later, I already had several businesses up, running, and making money. Even more would come. You are not beaten until you admit it. Hence, don't. It's all about the work.

CHAPTER 3

THE PERIL OF "POSITIVE THINKING"

DUMP THE "GOD COMPLEX"
AND START TALKING ABOUT FAILURE

TIME-OUT FOR A POP QUIZ ON A DOT-BOMB

NO ONE HAS AN ORIGINAL IDEA

ENCOURAGE INTELLIGENT FAILURE

MAKE SOFT LANDINGS

STOP TESTING AND START TRYING

CREATE A CULTURE OF KINDNESS, TRANSPARENCY,
RESPECT, AND—YES—LOVE

INNOVATION EVERY DAY—
THE SMALL-BUSINESS ADVANTAGE

THROW A FAILURE PARTY

B ack in 1952, the pastor of Manhattan's Marble
Collegiate Church, the Reverend Norman Vincent
Peale, published a book titled *The Power of Positive Thinking*. It became a runaway bestseller, and its main idea—that everything can be solved with optimism—took the country by storm, because it was a very American idea, and a very attractive one.

American optimism has launched many businesses. But it's all too easy for enthusiastic entrepreneurs to think that they can push through problems by sheer optimism. As I found out with Scrambler's Village, though, if you don't deal with reality, reality will surely deal with you.

There's actually recent scientific research to back up this personal experience of the perils of too much positivity. "(Too) Optimistic about Optimism: The Belief That Optimism Improves Performance," a study published in the March 2015 *Journal of Personality and Social Psychology*, found that most people believe (a) that optimism increases the likelihood of success, (b) that optimism encourages people to try harder, and (c) that optimism almost always improves performance. The study found, however, that optimism did not produce any measurable improvement at all. Nevertheless, propelled by the power of positive thinking, many business entrepreneurs recite such mantras as "I always stay positive!" or "No matter what, I always see the glass half full" or "The birds are always chirping and the sun is always shining." To listen to them, you would think their business is always perfect. Sales good? Wonderful! Always stay positive! Service failing? Wonderful! Always stay positive!

Business people who embrace the omnipotence of positive thinking are actually engaging in what psychologists call "magical thinking": all is well as long as I think all is well. Problem? Just give me a moment to think it away. It is the mental equivalent of too many Botox injections—a permanent smile that is both meaningless and grotesque. If you want your business to succeed, you cannot freeze yourself into the suspended animation of positive thinking.

In any business, even profitable, successful ones, there will always be bad news. Reach for it eagerly and deal with it, because bad news doesn't get better with age. Too many businesses have a corporate culture of treating failure as shameful and worthy of punishment, which creates a culture of not reporting, let alone dealing with, problems, a culture of burying the bad news as if it were a dead cat. I cannot tell you how many times I have done fellow entrepreneurs the great favor (because that is precisely what it is) of pointing out problems in their business, only to hear in response, "Oh, don't tell me that. I don't want to hear about it!" It would be comical if it weren't tragic.

Talking about "failure"—about what isn't working—is talking about truth and reality. But for the vast majority of businesses, *failure* is the F-word, never to be spoken out loud in polite company. That's simply wrong. I believe in talking about failure all the time, because the more I examine and ponder what didn't work, the more I can figure out what might work. One of the few—and greatest—businessmen I knew who openly talked about failure, and learning from it, was my friend Don Keough, who led the Coca-Cola Company through the infamous "New Coke" debacle. Don died in February 2015. He was quoted in his *New York Times* obituary as saying, "The word 'success' has always made me nervous, because I believe built into that word are a couple of viruses—arrogance and complacency—and left unchecked, they can ensure failure." That's exactly right—the kind of big failure you can avoid by learning from smaller failures.

Me as a Georgia Bulldog quarterback.

Number 10—that's me—with two of the NFL's greatest, Baltimore Colts MVP Johnny Unitas and Colts head coach Don Shula, at the 1965 Pro Bowl.

At the University of Georgia's Sanford Stadium some years back, positioned between two of the greatest players ever: on the left, Frank Sinkwich, Heisman Trophy winner at UGA, first-round draft pick with the NFL in the 1940s, and 1954 College Football Hall of Fame inductee; on the right, Charley Trippi, another 1940s UGA star, inducted into the College Football Hall of Fame in 1959 and the Pro Football Hall of Fame in 1968.

Bearing down on me fast, Number 87, Hall of Famer Claude Humphrey of the Atlanta Falcons.

With Bud Grant, the great head coach of the Minnesota Vikings and one of the most important influences on my career on and off the field.

Here I am—back row, fourth from left, with Bud Grant next to me, fifth from left—in 2013, one of the "50 Greatest Vikings Celebrating 50 Seasons."

One year, I teamed up with Y. A. Tittle (at right), the legendary Hall of Fame quarterback for the 49ers and New York Giants, to beat the tennis pros at a club doubles match on Sea Island. Amazingly enough, I do not remember the young woman on the left. (Honest.)

Kent McCord, as rookie LAPD cop Jim Reed, costarred opposite Martin Milner on TV's *Adam-12* (1968–1975). I met him when he was the real-life bodyguard for Rick Nelson, and we became great friends.

Me with my *That's Incredible!* cohosts Cathy Lee Crosby and John Davidson. John and I are good buddies to this day.

At Nashville's Grand Ole Opry, I shook hands with the late, great country western and rockabilly singer Ferlin Husky.

Next to me, second from the left, is two-time World Heavyweight Champion George Foreman having a few words with Peace Corps and Job Corps founder Sargent Shriver (next to George), who hired one of my early companies to create and conduct education programs in challenged neighborhoods. At the far right is Brooks Robinson, Hall of Fame third baseman for the Baltimore Orioles. We came to watch Foreman fight at Madison Square Garden. Like me, George is having a terrific life after professional sports—as an entrepreneur.

At center with the microphone is Mike Ditka, a legendary NFL player and for eleven years the iconic coach of the Chicago Bears, helping Sam Walton open a new Walmart not far from Chicago. "Mr. Sam," a man I revere as an entrepreneurial role model, stands in between Mike and me.

With media titan
Rupert Murdoch at
Nello, on Manhattan's
Upper East Side.

Both President George
W. Bush and I appeared
at the same technology
conference in New
Orleans.

In April 2015 I formally announced one of the Tarkenton Institute's latest ventures, the Tarkenton Certificate in Entrepreneurship, at the Athens Chamber of Commerce.

DUMP THE "GOD COMPLEX" AND START TALKING ABOUT FAILURE

The taboo against uttering the F-word grows stronger the closer you get to the top. In the mailroom, or in mid-management, you can bet they talk about problems in the business all the time. But as you rise to the C-suites, you find executives who think they have to hide behind the pretense that they are the smartest person in the room (except perhaps for their superiors). They feel they can't confess to failure, because they're expected to have all the answers. They adopt or exhibit a delusional "god complex," pretending to know all and see all—or, even worse, actually believing in their omniscience.

But here's where they're wrong (aside from their egos, and simply being delusional): talking about failure is recognizing reality, and as long as you come to grips with reality, you have a chance to succeed. More than that, talking about failure builds credibility with your team by demonstrating that you are not a leader who hides from the truth. By openly talking about failure, you model for your team the attitude and behavior you want from them: vigilance, a dynamic and continuous desire to improve, transparency, and straight talk. Finally, admitting and exploring a problem is an opportunity to build solidarity within the team. Telling your employees, "Our business is bad," is a dead end. Telling them, "Our business is bad. Help me fix it," is the beginning of success.

TIME-OUT FOR A POP QUIZ ON A DOT-BOMB

Question: What small business raised $375 million in a 1999 IPO, expanded from San Francisco to eight other American cities, placed a billion-dollar order with Bechtel—the world's largest construction company—for a set of cutting-edge warehouses, rose to a valuation of $1.2 billion (with stock at thirty dollars a share), and rolled out a twenty-six-city expansion plan—and did all of this in just eighteen months?

Answer: Webvan. Full name, Webvan.com, the Internet-based grocery store that offered customers the convenience of ordering food online and having it delivered within a thirty-minute window. Remember it? If you do, chances are you've either got a very good memory or you invested in the company. If Webvan had been a person, at least it would have left a headstone to mark its brief time on earth as a public company, a granite tablet carved with "RIP 1999–2001"—because at the end of those miraculous-seeming eighteen months in which Webvan rose from IPO to giant, it was dead. Commemorated by CNET in 2008 as the biggest dot-com flop in history, Webvan earned its place as yet another dot-bomb poster child, an extreme example of shoddy business at the turn of the millennium. Powered by positive thinking and (as it turned out) little else, the company hung its investors out to dry and tossed some two thousand employees onto the streets. Somehow, a company based on logistics hadn't figured out how to make its logistics work before splashing out on a mammoth, and in reality, unsustainable, infrastructure.

In 1999, the same year Webvan went public, day trading was all the rage. People who never before thought of themselves as investors were thoughtlessly but hopefully piling into the stock market, using their personal computer or a self-service terminal housed in a brokerage to buy and sell high-risk stocks, opening and closing trades on the same day. Their object was to exploit the fluctuations in especially volatile stocks in order to grab a quick profit. In their haste to buy into new companies, however, investors often overlooked the fundamentals of sound business

plans, reasonable market studies, and a realistic assessment of operating costs. Investors wildly bid up dot-com
stocks like Webvan only to see the bubbles burst. Reality
asserted itself, as it sooner or later always does. Between
September 1999 and October 2000, 117 dot-coms
imploded.

One lesson to learn from that is not to get swept away
with the crowd and not to invest in businesses you don't
understand or haven't fully studied. Don't let your optimism get in the way of your homework.

And don't let your optimism get in the way of immers-
ing yourself in the details of your business or your invest-
ments. This was hammered home to me about twenty
years ago when I read an interview with Oprah Winfrey.
Though she had a net worth of $800 million at the time
(which has since grown to some $3 billion), she confessed
to feeling powerless "all the time." She explained that,
over the years, she evolved a number of strategies and
tactics to overcome this feeling. The most important was
to embrace the principle of taking control of what you can.
She explained to the interviewer that she always signs all
of her company's checks. For a sole proprietor of a small
business, this is unremarkable. But Oprah reigns over an

empire! All the more reason she doesn't let anyone else sign her checks. She knows every nickel and dime her enterprises spend.

As soon as I read that interview, I started signing every check written by every one of my companies. Right away, I was stunned by how many errors I caught and also enlightened by discovering things for which I was paying too much as well as things on which I should have been spending more. Control what you can. Doing the small stuff will help you to grab hold of the big stuff. And don't invest in companies that, in their optimism, have skipped the small stuff.

NO ONE HAS AN ORIGINAL IDEA

For a solid example of true innovation, we can do no better than to turn to the most prolific innovator in American history, Thomas Alva Edison (1847 to 1931), who was awarded a record 1,093 U.S. patents, including patents for electric lighting and the phonograph.

As creative as he was, Edison readily admitted to making mistakes, but he also diligently learned from them. From his early teens, Edison made it a habit to carry a pocket notebook in which he jotted down ideas. In his laboratory-workshops, he placed notebooks on almost every horizontal surface, telling his employees to make meticulous notes for every experiment. He wanted everything, including every failure, recorded so he could learn from it. He also invited his employees to contribute their own ideas on the notebooks. When it came to inventing and innovating, he wanted to learn from everyone. And he worked harder than just about anyone, as was captured in his famous saying, "Genius is 1 percent inspiration and 99 percent perspiration."

I was surprised to learn that the idea for the phonograph started out with another invention, for which Edison filed a patent on March 13, 1876. In the patent papers, he called it an "Improvement in Autographic Printing." It was later marketed as the "electric pen," a handheld device that used a tiny reciprocating electric motor (the electric motor was something Edison had already invented!) to drive a needle very rapidly up and down. Edison thought it would be useful for creating stencils, which, in turn, would be a boon for reproducing documents and drawings; in fact, it became the basis for the mimeograph machine, analogue ancestor of today's digital copiers. But

Edison's *innovative* patent application for the electric pen refers to the *past*, to the use of stencils by the great fresco painters of the Renaissance, including Michelangelo. Edison related how his invention was based on the techniques of Renaissance artists and on those employed in the far more ancient craft of embroidery. In due course, what Edison learned from making the electric pen inspired him to adapt that technology, along with ideas taken from Alexander Graham Bell's patented telephone transmitter, to create the phonograph.

What are we to make of all this? Edison not only had an inventive and curious mind, and a well-stocked one, but he understood that every invention builds on the past.

No one has an original idea. Not Edison, not Steve Jobs, not Mark Zuckerberg. Every idea builds on ideas that went before it. We can expand our knowledge of ideas by observing, by reading, by talking to people, but we're never going to have an entirely original idea. It's what we do with the ideas that are out there that counts and that deserves to be called innovation.

Even Edison's most famous invention, the incandescent electric lamp, which was patented in 1879, was not a wholly original idea. Edison did not invent electric lighting. Sir

Humphry Davy, a famous British scientist, demonstrated an electric arc light in 1809, four decades before Edison was even born! Davy's light consisted of two charcoal rods wired to banks of sulfuric acid batteries. When the rods were drawn close to one another, a dazzling spark bridged the gap between the rods in a sizzling, hissing, brilliant arc. The problem was that this invention had no practical or commercial value. The batteries were unwieldy, hazardous, and quickly exhausted. As for the charcoal rods, they rapidly burned away. The life of the arc light was a matter of minutes.

Over the years, others tinkered, among them William Wallace, a full-time brass and copper founder who was also a part-time inventor. One day, in 1878, Edison visited his workshop, where Wallace showed him a version of an electric arc lamp system he had created with electrical inventor Moses Farmer. The lamps were nothing new, but Edison was impressed by the generator connected to them, which could power as many as eight lamps. Edison believed he could improve on the design and build a generator capable of lighting hundreds, even thousands of lamps; and the lamps themselves could be improved. Wallace's "intense light," he told a newspaper reporter, "had not been subdivided so that it could be brought into private houses."

So the inventor put it all together. Wallace and Farmer's generator energized Edison's thinking, enabling him to move beyond what those two inventors *had* accomplished to what they had *failed* to achieve, namely to "subdivide" light. In looking at those eight arc lamps illuminated by a single generator, Edison envisioned how electricity, a form of energy, could be retailed, like any other commodity, to hundreds of thousands, even millions, of consumers.

But what would make consumers want to buy electricity? Edison believed that people would pay good money to turn night into day with electric lighting. But first he had to find a way to "subdivide" the light into a form that was practical and safe for home users and that could be retailed to them. So he began the long, hard work of subdividing light by inventing a lamp that produced a glow more manageable, comfortable, practical, durable, and safe than that created by carbon arc technology.

As Edison knew it would, the incandescent electric lamp created a whole new utility industry—electrical

generation and distribution. He himself was at the fore-
front of inventing the hardware for this industry. Untold
millions of new jobs were created, not only to generate
and distribute power, but to invent and manufacture a
vast array of electrical appliances and devices. At the
same time, Edison's innovation disrupted many established industries: gas lighting companies, makers of
candles and kerosene lamps, and on and on. Innovation
brought both opportunity and failure in the form of
obsolescence. Economies, societies, and civilization were
transformed by the incandescent electric light, a spectacular innovation nevertheless based on no original
idea.

The complex sequence of innovations behind the electric power industry took time, imagination, commitment,
and hard work. Some people got rich, and others did not.
None of it happened in the span of a day trade. It was, as
Edison himself might have put it, a matter of persistence
and perspiration—with just a dash of vital inspiration.
Electric light and electric power took hold and transformed
civilization not because it was a get-rich-quick proposition,
but because it created and offered enormous value.

ENCOURAGE INTELLIGENT FAILURE

We talk about "trial and error" but it's really "trial and failure." As we learned in chapter 1, Edison tested some ten thousand materials before he identified a practical filament for his lamp. It was a time-consuming and exhausting process, and when a reporter asked him if he was discouraged at having failed ten thousand times, the inventor replied, "I have not failed. I've just found ten thousand ways that won't work."

Edison proudly boasted that he never permitted himself "to become discouraged under any circumstances." After performing "thousands of experiments on a certain project without solving the problem," one of Edison's technicians complained about having failed "to find out anything." Edison responded "that we *had* learned something ... [the] certainty that the thing couldn't be done that way, and that we would have to try some other way."

The inventor was not being flip. He believed that any experiment that yielded data was successful, whether or not the result was also immediately profitable. We "sometimes learn a lot from our failures," he said, provided that "we have put into the effort the best thought and work we are capable of." Both lazy and hardworking people fail. The difference is that if you work hard enough to achieve your failure, you are likely to get something valuable out of it.

MAKE SOFT LANDINGS

As an employer, Thomas Edison was no bleeding heart. He worked long hours, often substituting catnaps curled up on a lab table for a full night's sleep in bed at home. While he never explicitly demanded that his employees follow his example, the example was set nevertheless, and his "boys" got the message. But while Edison would not tolerate laziness in his employees, he showed infinite tolerance for failure—provided that it was *intelligent* failure, failure that produced carefully recorded results, whether positive or negative.

The global design company IDEO says of itself, "We create impact through design." Aiming to be a leader in design, IDEO puts the emphasis on innovation. As Mark D. Cannon and Amy C. Edmondson observe in their article in *Long Range Planning*, "Failing to Learn and Learning to Fail (Intelligently): How Great Organizations Put Failure to Work to Innovate and Improve," innovation requires not only giving employees permission to fail but positively encouraging them to do so. Internally, IDEO communicates "with slogans such as *'Fail often in order to succeed sooner'* and *'Enlightened trial-and-error succeeds over the planning of the lone genius.'* These sayings are accompanied by frequent small experiments, and much good humor about associated failures [emphasis mine]."

Some companies extend the policy of intelligent failure to employee development and career. PSS/World Medical has what it calls a "soft-landing policy," which means, according to Cannon and Edmondson, that "if an employee tries out a position, but does not succeed after a good faith effort, the employee can have his or her former job back." I think "soft-landing policy" is a good label to paste on any business model that not only allows but encourages failure—intelligent failure, the failure that sometimes results from "good faith" efforts, whether it's trying a new idea concerning a product, service, or method, or trying out a new job.

Remember something called the "Peter Principle"? Management guru Laurence J. Peter coined it in the title of his 1969 bestseller, *The Peter Principle: Why Things*

Always Go Wrong. In a nutshell, the Peter Principle states that corporations promote employees based on their performance in their current position, which means that promotion stops only after an employee has stopped performing effectively; therefore "managers rise to the level of their incompetence" and stay there. Admittedly, the Peter Principle theory of management does have a ring to it, and it is certainly good for a cynical chuckle. Contrary to what many seem to think, however, the Peter Principle was not chiseled on a stone tablet and carried down from a mountaintop. Yes, employees sometimes try a different career path or get promoted only to fail in their new position. But what corporate god decreed that they must *either* stay forever in that position, doomed to fail forever, *or* be fired?

STOP TESTING AND START TRYING

Isn't taking a chance with a soft landing better than surrendering to the Peter Principle?

Many might answer not just *No*, but *Hell, no!* They will tell you that what's "better" is not to try in the first place, but instead to give the employee an exhaustive battery of aptitude and personality tests prepared by experts. Surely, these will prevent the failure before you promote the employee!

While this response sounds like common sense, it is actually a symptom of a particularly serious case of the god complex because it makes the delusional assumption that an employer can accurately determine *in advanc*e if an employee will succeed or fail in a new position. True, some predictions can be made. But the only way to *know* for sure is to try. And the only way to try without risking disaster for either the company or the employee is to give that employee permission to fail, a permission bundled with a "soft landing" alternative to permanent failure (rising to the level of incompetence and staying there forever) or unemployment.

As for "personality" and "aptitude" tests used as hiring tools, I've had quite a bit of experience with them. Back in 1962, after my rookie season with the Vikings, Wilson Trucking Systems gave me a personality test before hiring me at $600 a month, and, later, when I was working with Dr. Aubrey Daniels, bringing "performance management" to the textile mills of the South during the 1970s, I called on company after company that routinely administered the tests. To me, it seemed obvious that the tests were not reliably predictive. For most companies, administering the tests, expensive as they were, was more a matter of routine and ritual than of useful research.

As far as I can tell, this is still the case. The classic Myers-Briggs Type Indicator (MBTI) is taken by 2.5 million people a year and is used by human resources departments in eighty-nine of the Fortune 100 companies. Adam Grant, the youngest-tenured and highest-rated professor at the Wharton School of the University of Pennsylvania, is the author of *Give and Take*, a *New York Times* and *Wall Street Journal* bestseller about how we interact with each other. I had the pleasure of talking with him for our Business Mentoring Series on my GoSmallBiz.com website. In a blog post for HuffPost Business, Professor Grant called the MBTI "the fad that won't die." He wrote that the test identified him as an "INTJ," which means that he is "more introverted than extraverted, intuiting than sensing, thinking than feeling, and judging than perceiving." When he took the *same* test just a few months later, however, he was classified as an "ESFP"—an extrovert. "Suddenly, I had become the life of the party, the guy who follows his heart and throws caution to the wind." This led him to ask, "Had my personality changed, or is the test not all it's cracked up to be?"

In a 2002 article published in the *University of Pennsylvania Journal of Labor and Employment Law* titled "The Use of Personality Tests as a Hiring Tool: Is the Benefit Worth the Cost?," law professor Susan J. Stabile concluded that "employers often make hiring decisions on the basis of personality tests that, in many cases, do not do what they are supposed to do, discriminate against certain job applicants, and invade the privacy of all applicants." Stabile advised decreasing "reliance on personality tests and improv[ing] the tests that are used." A reasonable recommendation, but doesn't it make even more sense to find ways to give employees a "soft landing" so that they can actually *try* new things? The employer and employee may discover great benefits, or few benefits, or outright failure. Whatever the result, both employer and employee will have actually tried and therefore actually learned—and all without ruining the life of an employee or the health of the company.

CREATE A CULTURE OF KINDNESS, TRANSPARENCY, RESPECT, AND—YES—LOVE

In 1989, the 101st Congress passed what is popularly called the Whistleblower Protection Act, designed to encourage federal workers to report violations of law or regulations, gross mismanagement, waste of funds, abuse of authority, or dangers to health or safety in the federal agencies in which they work. The act protects whistleblowers against retaliation for reporting problems and misconduct.

Remember that old saying *Don't shoot the messenger*? Well, the Whistleblower Protection Act is an attempt to keep public-sector messengers from being shot. Its spirit and intention are well worth emulating in the private sector. You can never know *enough* about your business, and there is no such thing as knowing *too much* about your business. All information and insight is good news, especially when it is bad news. Because the sooner you know what's going wrong, the sooner you can act to fix it or at least to contain the damage.

You should always invite comments from employees, vendors, customers, friends—everyone who has any contact with your company. Make it clear that you're not fishing for compliments, and be sure the other person knows how much you value his assessment, insight, and opinion. "Ralph, how can we deliver better service to you? I value your opinion. I need your insight. What's working for you and what isn't?" And when you get a frank response—maybe a harsher, more critical response than you bargained for—suppress your natural urge to respond defensively ("That's unfair!") or with denial ("Nobody's ever complained about *that* before."). Instead, convey heartfelt thanks and ask for more: "Ralph, thank you for being so honest and direct about this. Please give me all the gory details. I want to fix this!"

Believe it or not, it's pretty hard to get people to criticize or complain to *you* about something for which *you* are responsible. ("The Thanksgiving turkey you spent all day preparing tasted just like cardboard, Mom.") While the last thing you want to do is create a workplace in which people habitually grumble, gripe, and whine, you *do* want to move heaven and earth to create a culture of kindness, transparency, respect, and—why not use the L-word?—love.

Fortunately, creating such a culture is both joyful and rewarding. When it comes to kindness, it is simply more fun to be kind than it is to be mean. Kindness means treating people as colleagues, rather than as tools to be used or as dogs to be scolded or as potential threats to one's god complex.

Part of being collegial is being honest. The buzzword for honesty these days is *transparency*. Sure, some businesses at least some of the time have a need for confidentiality, especially if they are in a high-tech space or other market sector that depends on trade secrets and the like. Negotiations are also often sensitive. So, while "transparency" doesn't mean you have to expose everything to full view by everyone, it does mean keeping secrets to a minimum and always dealing aboveboard to create and maintain a culture of plain dealing and honesty—transparency. It is a fact in business as well as in government that relatively few matters actually require secrecy. It is also true that most people accept the need for a certain amount of confidentiality. In fact, it is not secrecy to which they object, but opacity and obscurity—the failure to explain what is perfectly explicable or to account for what should be accounted for. People object to the feeling that the company—or the government—is hiding things for the sake of hiding them and is therefore fundamentally untrustworthy or untrusting or, most likely, both.

In your dealings with customers, employees, investors, or the public at large, pare down your secrets to the absolute minimum. Emulate some of the world's finest restaurants, which, instead of walling off their kitchen in the backroom, put it on display behind a counter or glass. Take pride in the inner workings of your enterprise. Take time to explain policies, practices, and procedures. Set clarity as both a high-priority goal and a nonnegotiable value.

Respect means more than courtesy, it means following the Golden Rule. Most of us know it as "Do unto others as you would have them do unto you," which is paraphrased from the New Testament, Matthew 7:12. But this "ethic of reciprocity" is a virtue and a value nearly universally recognized in all religions and cultures. Basically, you can't go wrong with respect as defined by the Golden Rule. As part of that, we should seek out and listen to what our employees and customers have to say, welcoming their comments rather than stifling them or belittling them. As a business leader, you need to know as much as you can from as many people as you can. So respect your employees and customers and encourage them to talk to you. You want to find ways to innovate at your business? That's where you'll find them.

INNOVATION EVERY DAY—THE SMALL-BUSINESS ADVANTAGE

McKinsey & Company is a consulting giant with more than a hundred offices worldwide and some seventeen thousand employees. Its clients are the planet's biggest, richest companies, which is why some might find it surprising that a McKinsey blog published a recent article that began, "It's almost conventional wisdom that innovation springs from developers and entrepreneurs based in start-up hubs such as Silicon Valley." In other words, the McKinsey blogger thought that the prospect of innovation happening among corporate giants was so unusual that it was worth writing about.

The truth is this. *Any* company of *any* size can develop a culture that encourages innovation, even on a daily basis. To do this, however, such a company must also encourage failure—especially intelligent failure—every day. And in this, *small* businesses, especially start-ups, definitely have the edge. They have the advantage of not being shackled to the status quo. With literally less to lose but proportionately more to gain, entrepreneurial start-ups can "fail faster better" than the blue-chip behemoths. In fact, entrepreneurs, especially those who lead start-ups, are not only freer to innovate, they have no choice but to do so.

THROW A FAILURE PARTY

So stop envying the big market leaders and simply enjoy out-innovating them. Even McKinsey, darling of the Fortune 500, admits you have the advantage. As for the failures that accompany acts of innovation, I can't offer a formula for avoiding them. That's because you cannot avoid them, and you should not, even if you could. Failure is integral to innovation.

You can, however, take the sting out of failure by emulating one of a very tiny handful of big companies that enthusiastically embrace both innovation and failure. Writing in *Harvard Business Review* ("Strategies for Learning from Failure," April 2011), Amy C. Edmondson reports that big pharma icon Eli Lilly has long been reducing "the stigma of failure" by throwing "'failure parties' to honor intelligent, high-quality scientific experiments that fail to achieve the desired results." Inexpensive in itself, a failure party not only honors effort and acknowledges the acquisition of valuable data, it also doubles as a kind of launch party to kick off the redeployment of "valuable resources—particularly scientists—to new projects" as quickly as possible. Partying to launch a new effort is a lot better than wasting time in hand wringing and finger pointing. Lilly has been throwing these failure

parties since the early 1990s, but I just bet that any entrepreneurial start-up could out-party even that $23 billion
S&P 500 A-lister. Celebrate the failure. Then use it to
build your next—or your very first—success.

CHAPTER 4

BREAK SOME EGGS

MAKE 1 PLUS 1 EQUAL 3

GET ALL THE PARTNERS YOU NEED

MAKE SURE YOUR PARTNERS MAKE MONEY

KNOW WHEN TO MOVE ON—THEN GET MOVING

ASK WHAT'S NEXT

IF YOUR BUSINESS HAS LEGS, KEEP ON RIDING IT

"Why didn't *I* think of that?"

That's what everybody—and I mean *everybody*—said back in the early 1980s, when I launched Ticket Marketing Inc. But though creating the company was, if I say so myself, an impressive achievement, and though it had been fun, even if I had worked harder to keep it going, even if I had successfully built on our initial success, *not every success is successful.* Why is that? Well, because in the case of Ticket Marketing Inc., we would have been made obsolete by the e-ticket. When you're in business, when you're an entrepreneur, you need to know that your great ideas are vulnerable to new and better ideas. You need to be prepared. You need to constantly look ahead. You need to see how the eventual *failure* of your idea could lead to a better idea.

MAKE 1 PLUS 1 EQUAL 3

Obsolescence and innovation go hand in hand. Edison's friend and fellow inventor Alexander Graham Bell once said, "When one door closes, another opens; but we often look so long and so regretfully upon the closed door that we do not see the one which has opened for us." As an athlete, a businessman, and a human being, I've never believed in wasting time staring at closed doors. Instead, I go out to find the doors that have opened. *That* is what all true entrepreneurs do. In the early 1980s, the doors of the digital age—the era whose innovations would eventually make businesses like Ticket Marketing Inc. irrelevant—were just beginning to open. I was never a techie, not a Steve Jobs or a Bill Gates, not even close. But I saw the signs, and, in particular, I was hearing a lot about a thing called CASE, computer-aided software engineering. As I've proudly admitted to you, I've never had a truly original idea—no more than Tom Edison did. Every business idea I've developed has been developed by talking with others and listening to them: customers, experts, leaders of other companies, anyone who will share their experience and insight with me. So when people I admired were talking about CASE, I looked deeper and decided to buy into it. It made sense. If computers were designing more and more of the world around me, why shouldn't computers be used to design the software that was designing the modern world?

Writing software code is a labor-intensive, time-consuming enterprise. In the 1980s, it was a handicraft, really, just as building an automobile had been before Henry Ford transformed the process into an industry with his assembly line. I found and met with a New York–based software developer who was working on software that automated a key aspect of creating other software. It was a code generator he called Gamma. The trouble was that he'd run out of money. Well, for him, that was trouble. For an entrepreneur like me, it was opportunity. I didn't convene a board meeting or huddle with consultants. After talking with the developer, I was convinced. I broke the egg and started making my omelet.

I took over Gamma, funded it, and brought its developer down to Atlanta, along with some of his people. They would become the tech core of Tarkenton Software, which I started in 1982. Even if I had wanted a loan to start the new company, I doubt any bank would have put up the money. I had, after all, no experience in the software industry. And I didn't want a loan, because Scrambler's Village had taught me the perils of debt. To launch Tarkenton Software, I took $3 million from my other businesses, which allowed us to start debt-free.

Aided by a sales force of three, I peddled Gamma wherever I could. We did sell some units. In fact, we sold just about enough installations of Gamma to lose a lot of money. What this fact told me was that we couldn't go it alone, and so I looked for a partner.

For many aspiring entrepreneurs, one of the attractions is building a business singlehandedly. The prospect is exciting, romantic—like being a lone pioneer on the Old West frontier. If you are romantically inclined in this direction, my advice is that you actually read some Western non-fiction. What you'll discover is that most *lone* pioneers went back home—or died on the frontier. To create a viable business without help is nearly impossible. To sustain one is absolutely impossible. Sooner or later, you need a partner, typically more than one. Unlike many of my fellow entrepreneurs, I didn't have to learn this the hard way. My sports were baseball, basketball, and, of course, football. For me, teamwork was second nature.

So I met with companies—so many, in fact, that I can't even remember them all by name. Among the CEOs I met was one who pointed me to a potential partner, a man named James Martin. "You really need to meet him," he said.

When James Martin died in June 2013 at the age of seventy-nine, he was honored in obituaries as a visionary technologist, futurologist, and educational philanthropist.

Thirty years earlier, when I met him, he was already a legend in the computer industry (though I had never heard of him before I was directed to him by that CEO). Martin had pioneered real-time online computer systems at IBM during the late 1950s, including SABRE, the reservation software that became the global standard among commercial airlines. He had made a fortune from developing software, writing computer and software textbooks, offering high-level executive seminars, and his consulting firm. He was a tech guru and a profound thinker who endowed Oxford University with some $150 million to create, in 2005, the Oxford Martin School, a center for the interdisciplinary study of the future.

If, in 1982, I had no idea who James Martin was, my tech guys sure did. After talking with them, my next step was clear. I called Martin's office. One of his assistants told me that Martin would be finishing a seminar in Dallas on Saturday morning and could meet me then and there. I arranged a flight, landed in Dallas, and sat in on the tail end of the seminar—hearing more than enough to be thoroughly impressed with the man's brilliance and charisma. Martin was a visionary and financier, not a day-to-day manager, not a hands-on maker. He started companies and relied on others to execute his vision. My technology team had briefed me on a company Martin had founded in Ann Arbor, Michigan, to build the "front end" components of CASE, tools for design and analysis. He originally called the company Database Design, but by the time I met him he had renamed it KnowledgeWare. In Gamma, we were working on the complementary "back end" of the CASE process: a code generator.

I had lunch with Martin and told him all about Gamma. I was just getting to the part where I was going to explain how I saw his company's front end as the perfect complement to our back end in what, if we partnered, we could market as a *complete* CASE solution. But before the words were out of my mouth, it was clear that he was way ahead of me. He saw what I saw, and the possibilities appealed to him.

What we had in common were companies with unrealized potential. Like Tarkenton Software, KnowledgeWare was struggling. We were both pioneering CASE, but neither of us had the complete CASE solution. I had my tech team, a great product, my own strategic skillset, and a small sales force. Martin had a terrific technical team and a connection with the highly respected Arthur Young, the accounting and business consulting firm that would soon become Ernst & Young, the blue-chip consultancy that now calls itself EY. At the time I met with Martin, the Arthur Young firm was furiously developing an IT consulting practice to compete with its industry rival, Arthur Andersen. So each of us, clearly, brought much to the table. Here was an opportunity to build the kind of 1+1=3 leverage a truly effective partnership creates.

We closed a deal fast—in a matter of weeks. I moved Martin's company, lock, stock, and engineers, to Atlanta. (After many Viking winters in Minneapolis, *I* was not about to move north to Ann Arbor!) Along with Martin's people, I took his company's name. I'm proud of my name, which has opened any number of doors for me. But I didn't need to be convinced that "KnowledgeWare" was more compelling as a brand label for a software company than "Tarkenton." It simply said more. And so, in 1986, Tarkenton Software was reborn in our Atlanta offices as KnowledgeWare.

GET ALL THE PARTNERS YOU NEED

Separately, my company and Martin's had been struggling. Instead of giving up, we found a partial solution in a partnership that resulted in my buying his company. Then, in 1987, Arthur Young made a modest but welcome investment in our combined company and also reached into its accounting practice in Atlanta and identified one of its own people to serve as our CFO. This allowed me to connect with Young's top leadership—a good thing for moving the partnership closer to that 1+1=3 equation. But often you require even more, so you go out and get all the partners you need. I wanted to build a strong relationship with Arthur Young, whose accounting and consulting credibility would really help us build our brand. When the new CFO decided he needed help, he called in another Arthur Young guy, Rick Gossett, who was already based in Atlanta. It was immediately apparent to me that Rick was a great addition to our company, and, in fact, he never left us. Today, he is the COO of Tarkenton Companies.

With its investment and two of its people, Arthur Young now had a toe in the KnowledgeWare pond. But I wanted more than a toe. I wanted that company as a *partner*, right there in the deep water with us. Soon, we had them using our products in the work they did for their consulting clients. We also made them the exclusive distributor of our software in Europe. Establishing these two relationships meant more revenue, of course, but it also let KnowledgeWare bask in the halo of a distinguished blue-chip consulting brand, it introduced us to many of the great firms Arthur Young served, and it gave our small company a global footprint. We soon opened European offices—in London, Paris, and Germany. Now that we *all* had skin in the game, Arthur Young's participation became another 1+1=3 partnership.

So things were looking up, way up. But it was still apparent to me that something was missing in our basic CASE offering. I'd started with a code generator—the back end of a CASE solution. Thanks to James Martin, I had added planning and analysis tools: the front end. As I said, I'm no technologist. But I do know that a front end and a back end need something in between: a middle. To offer the world a truly complete CASE solution, we needed a package that combined planning and analysis (the front end) and code generation (the back end), with a software design component between the two. With this three-part sequence, you could automate the *entire* development process: from planning and analysis to design, to churning out the code that was the finished piece of software.

So we began working on the middle, and we had a design module ready to go by 1988. Now that we had the complete package, I believed we needed yet another partner to help us put it out into the software industry in a big way. The time had come to make a grand red carpet entrance, not just to sneak quietly into the marketplace. So I sat down with our chief technical officer (CTO), Mike Ryan.

"We need more partnerships," I declared to him.

"Well, IBM would be a great partner."

It seemed to me he was dreaming. I mean, in 1988 IBM was still synonymous with *The* Computer. It was the Ford, Chrysler, GM, and Rolls-Royce of the industry. And it was a massive company, a nuclear-powered aircraft carrier whose passing wake would, I thought, swamp our little sailboat. Why would IBM even care about us? But Mike persisted.

"I'm serious. IBM *made* Microsoft and Intel, which are big companies now because IBM needed them when they were little companies. Our CASE package is something IBM needs. We just have to let them know."

I was far from convinced, but to make an omelet, you do have to break some eggs. Besides, I saw approaching IBM, Big Blue, as a challenge. If I was rebuffed, yes, there would be egg on my face, but so what? I had hired Mike Ryan to advise me on technology. Now he was advising me to call IBM. I had successfully faced truck-sized tackles and millions of *Saturday Night Live* viewers. I could sure as hell get on the phone now with IBM chairman John Akers and make a damn fool of myself.

So I made the call, and when Akers answered, I introduced myself—"Fran Tarkenton. I used to play football."—as if that could mean anything to him.

"I know who you are." The response was a surprise. "What can I do for you?" An even bigger surprise.

"I'm embarrassed to call you, but I've got this technology guy who thinks we've got something you would be interested in. But any time you want to hang up on me, please do, because I believe he's crazy. I think last year, John, we did about $2 million in software sales. You probably do a little bit more than that at IBM." He laughed: a good sign. "We have a CASE product that my tech guy thinks would be compatible with your technology. And just to shut him up, I'd like to get in front of one of your engineers with it and let him tell me to go to hell."

"No, no. I'd be happy to gather a *group* of our people to listen to you, Fran. I'd like to see what you're doing."

Soon after I hung up, I grabbed Mike Ryan—together with a dozen footballs (I keep a lot of footballs in my office)—bundled us into my Lear 35, and flew up to the airport in White Plains, New York, a short car ride from IBM headquarters in Armonk. There, the two of us were led into a room in which twenty engineers were gathered.

Looking at their unsmiling faces, I knew just what they were thinking. *What in the hell? We've got to sit here and listen to this ex-jock gas on about "technology," something he obviously knows nothing about?* So I set my bag full of footballs down, motioned for Mike to take a seat, pulled an old windup stopwatch out of my pocket, and set it on the table.

"First of all, I want to apologize to all of you for your having to be here. I'm sure you were told you had to be here to listen to some ex–football jock tell you about his gee-whiz technology, and you know better than to expect anything remotely resembling a gee-whiz. So, two things I want to offer you. Number one, I've got these footballs with me, which I'll autograph for you or your kids. And if more of you want footballs, I'll autograph them in Atlanta and send them up overnight. Second, I've got a stopwatch here. I'm going to take exactly thirty minutes of your time. After exactly thirty minutes are up, I'm walking out of here. So I'll thank you in advance for your thirty minutes and make my apologies for wasting them right now."

After the giggles, I introduced Mike and let him do his thing. As soon as the stopwatch hit thirty minutes, I got up, cut Mike off, and turned to the engineers.

"Thank you so much ..."

"No, no, no, no. We want to hear more."

We were there for three hours. Two weeks later, we hosted a delegation of IBMers in Atlanta.

"You know," one of them told me, "what you've built is a repository for software development. This is what we've been trying to do—build a repository with all the development tools, and here you've got *the* CASE repository. With it, we can go out and help people build the custom applications they need. We really are interested."

The next thing you know, we had a $10 million investment from IBM—which we didn't ask for, but which we happily accepted—and a blue-chip partner to sell our product all over the world. Bottom line? We took KnowledgeWare from $2 million in 1988 to $129 million by 1991. In 1991, we were ranked by *BusinessWeek* as number 2 in a list of "hot-growth" companies. We had gone public in 1989 at $12.50 a share. In 1991, shares were selling for $43.

MAKE SURE YOUR PARTNERS MAKE MONEY

The moral of the KnowledgeWare story—at least up to 1991—is the Power of the Partnership. IBM was a great partner, as I told anyone who asked. Many were surprised by this. Some executives and entrepreneurs I spoke with complained that their partnership experiences with Big Blue never worked out for them. A few even said that IBM had been a terrible partner.

"Really?" I responded. "What did they do?"

Invariably, I did not get much of an explanation, just a repetition of the lament. So I went on: "I found out very quickly that IBM liked to make money. Imagine that! IBM liked to make money just as much as I do. They didn't go into the partnership to make money for *me*. They went into it to make money for *IBM*. So I made sure that they had the right equity and the right commissions. In fact, I made sure that *they* made money before *I* made money. And the partnership, it took care of itself—and, pretty soon, it took care of us."

IBM made money. We made money. We built a great company. All thanks to real value, a solid partnership, and good technology. But then the technology did what technology always does. It changed. It changed everything, again.

KNOW WHEN TO MOVE ON— THEN GET MOVING

As you probably know, IBM hired the fledgling Microsoft Corporation to make an operating system for the personal computer—the "PC"—it was inventing. IBM allowed Microsoft to retain ownership of the software, called DOS (disk operating system), and Microsoft, in return, formed a partnership with IBM in 1980 that allowed it to bundle DOS with IBM computers. In 1985, IBM asked Microsoft to create a new operating system for its computers, to be called OS/2. Microsoft built it, but it also developed and sold an alternative, Windows, which it released the very same year. Windows had a lot of growing pains, but it not only proved to be a direct competitor with OS/2, it quickly overtook OS/2 in sales. In fact, by the 1990s, Windows captured more than 90 percent of the operating system market.

Our powerful partner, the principal driver of our sales, IBM was locked in mortal combat with the very company whose fortune it had made. In many ways, OS/2 was a remarkable technical achievement, especially in offering the best features of Unix without the geeky baggage that came with it. This enabled multitasking on a level that

DOS just could not reach. But OS/2 could not compete with Windows, no matter how hard IBM pushed it. In the course of combat, IBM decided to migrate our CASE products to OS/2. That move not only failed to boost sales of IBM's declining operating system, it doomed our software. Adding salt to our wound was the fact that IBM, the creator of the modern personal computer, came to regard the PC as a kind of Frankenstein's monster, a menace to its long-established mainframe computer business. The result was one of the great ironies of the modern technology industry: the instigator of the client-server revolution fell victim to that revolution. And so did our CASE software. The front end was designed to work on the PC, but the code generated by the back end was written in COBOL, the venerable language of "big iron," the IBM mainframes. The combination of migration to OS/2 and code outputted in COBOL drove a stake through the heart of our product, which became irrelevant in a world rushing away from mainframes and into the arms of Windows-based client-server systems.

And it all happened practically overnight—not just to little KnowledgeWare, but to Big Blue itself. Having missed the client-server revolution it started, IBM was thrown into a turmoil that resulted in (among other things) the ouster of chairman John Akers, our champion.

There was no question of our undertaking a massive reengineering project to rescue our software. It did not make business sense. The only alternative to complete disaster, therefore, was to sell KnowledgeWare. In doing this, I didn't dare hope for a touchdown. I just didn't want to get kicked out of the stadium. In search of a buyer for my company, I did what I had so often done before: knocked on doors, a whole lot of doors, the last two of which (after so many) belonged to software giant Computer Associates (CA) and a smaller company, Sterling Software. CA at first appeared to be a highly promising prospect. When its enthusiasm fizzled, however, the much smaller Sterling loomed as my last dance partner.

We began engaging with Sterling in the spring of 1994, and by the fall of that year, we closed the sale for $100 million. Now, KnowledgeWare had been worth five times that amount at its peak. Stock that had traded at twenty-three dollars a share was sold for five dollars, but I was grateful for the sale nonetheless. Better than nothing? Actually, it turned out to be *much* better. With the sale, I remained on the company's board, and I took my proceeds in stock rather than cash. In 1999, not long after it made the purchase, Sterling split itself, selling one unit (as Sterling Software) to Computer Associates and the other (as Sterling Commerce) to Southwestern Bell. Each half of the company sold for about $3.5 billion, which made the shares I still held worth a lot more than the sale price of my company.

The client-server revolution and the emergence of Windows had made our CASE software irrelevant, one innovation rendering another obsolete. You cannot build your business on a single unchanging product or technology and expect it to outlast the pyramids. But if you see the signs, read the signs, and act on them in a timely fashion, you can still win and live to fight another day. I found a buyer. I made money. And my buyer, Sterling, made money—selling itself just before the dot-com boom became the dot-bomb bust as the twentieth century turned into the twenty-first.

ASK WHAT'S NEXT

By 1994, when we sold it, KnowledgeWare was the principal business of Tarkenton Companies. My partners and I had had a good run with the company, and, with the sale to Sterling, I made the exit from KnowledgeWare work. Most entrepreneurs put all their thinking into how to enter a business, but how you exit from one is just as important as how you enter it. Although I could not have known it back in 1994, the 1999 Sterling sales to Computer Associates and Southwestern Bell would result in a tripling of my stock holdings in the company I sold. Some people excel at making a grand entrance. I pulled off a grand exit!

Although I had gone out on a financial high note, I had to deal with the fact that my main business was no longer mine. I was fifty-four in 1994. That's an age when many consider a comfortable retirement the ultimate sign of success. For me, however, nothing was further from my mind, heart, soul, and gut. I was and am an entrepreneur. There always comes a time to change a business, to sell or even simply end a business. When it came time to exit KnowledgeWare, I scrambled to make a decent sale, and I sold the company without a single regret, because my attention immediately shifted to what I would do next.

Whatever new business I started, I didn't have to start from zero. I could build on the experience and brand equity Tarkenton Companies had built in the technology sector. I took to my Lear 35 and called on hardware maker Hewlett-Packard and software maker Oracle. I even had a sit-down with Steve Jobs, who, having been pushed out of Apple, the company he'd founded, was now CEO of Pixar and NeXT Computer. When I talked with him, he was set up in a small, nondescript office, not only typical of modest start-ups throughout the suburbs of Silicon Valley, but much like the strip mall headquarters in which he had brought to birth the world-changing Mac back in 1984. That was a dumpy building distinguished only by the Jolly Roger pirate flag Jobs flew over it.

Then I called on Steve Ballmer, who in 1996, when I met with him, was executive vice president, sales and support, for the Microsoft Corporation. He was very interested in expanding Microsoft's reach to small businesses, which, Ballmer told me, were underserved by big businesses, Microsoft included.

My meeting with Steve Ballmer gave me an idea. The U.S. Small Business Administration tells us that small businesses make up

- 99.7 percent of U.S. employer firms,
- 64 percent of net new private-sector jobs,
- 49.2 percent of private-sector employment,

- 42.9 percent of private-sector payroll,
- 46 percent of private-sector output,
- 43 percent of high-tech employment,
- 98 percent of firms exporting goods, and
- 33 percent of exporting value.

My partners and I did not think of ourselves as small-business people. We thought of ourselves as entrepreneurs, and our customers and partners had always been big companies, all members of the Fortune 1000. But now I saw that there could be a great opportunity, a great future, a great need filled by partnering with small business.

I became a man with a mission. I told my COO, Rick Gossett, "We've got to help small businesses." The question was how we could best do that.

I not only started researching small business and its needs, but, in 1996, I broke my first egg in the small-business frying pan by starting a new company, Fran Tarkenton Small Business Network (FTSBN), which we intended as a service provider for small businesses. I also looked for partners to help us. Our first substantive meeting was in the New Jersey offices of Dun & Bradstreet, which was putting together a product they called Business in a Box.

Business in a Box—now *that* seemed to pretty well describe what we wanted to offer: a bundle of discounts on software, rental cars, hotels, financial services, and so on. Rick and I hoped to develop a partnership with D&B to collaborate on a "box" that would be bigger and better than either of us could create separately.

In the meantime, I started talking to small-business people in what I dubbed a "listening tour" across much of the country. I discovered that many were sole proprietors, often running the classic mom-and-pop operation. I also discovered that many were being taken advantage of by hucksters touting fantastic "biz ops"—surefire, can't-miss business opportunities from which a flow of instant wealth was virtually inevitable. Many of these "biz ops" were network marketing schemes, in which members bought merchandise at wholesale to sell at a markup, but actually spent most of their time and effort recruiting more members. Now, don't get me wrong, some biz ops and some network marketing enterprises are good companies that offer legitimate opportunities. But I was shocked to find that most were built on sheer hype. I had been naïve enough to think that the days of the traveling medicine show peddling snake oil had ended with the era of P. T. Barnum. No way. Every day, tens of thousands—hundreds of thousands—of people aspiring to run their own businesses were gathering in hotel and motel conference rooms and ballrooms all across the country listening to latter-day carnival barkers hawking the latest elixir. The hucksters could prey on these hard-working small-business people, because the mom-and-pop owners of businesses that employed one to ten workers did not have access to the services, products, business advice, and expert knowledge that bigger businesses take for granted. I wanted to change that.

In the end, we were unable to form a partnership with Dun & Bradstreet. It was probably just as well, because my listening tour through small-business America persuaded me that simply putting together a "box" of products was not a big enough mission for us. To really help small businesses, to give them the access to the services and knowledge they needed, we had to think outside of that box.

At this time, the Internet was just emerging as an extraordinary and unprecedented network of networks.

The Internet offered something bigger and better than a box. It offered a dynamic means of real-time distribution of products and ideas as well as a vast network of connections. Where a box was inert, the technology of connectivity was *alive*.

I started talking with a new class of entrepreneur, digital marketers. One company in particular was a technology design firm that built websites for businesses of all kinds. We asked them to build a site for FTSBN—and then it occurred to me that, if they could build a website for us to reach out to our small-business customers, why couldn't they build a product that would help small businesses build their own websites for themselves? Remarkably, they had never thought of this before. But yes, they responded, they *could* put their web-building tools on a CD-ROM, which they could wholesale to us and we could sell as part of our now increasingly web-based business in a box. Ultimately, we decided to add the CD-ROM to our box without charging extra for it. The income for us and our software partner would come from the monthly fees the small businesses would pay for hosting the websites they created using the tools provided. We hired the software guys, added some people to their staff, set them up in an office, and put them to work creating the CD product. Not only did we distribute the software in our own box, we sold some units to software retailers such as Egghead.

It was terrific—while it lasted. But it didn't last long. No sooner were we out in the marketplace than Microsoft released its website development tool, FrontPage, and we soon felt the pressure of the furry foot of an eight-hundred-pound gorilla.

IF YOUR BUSINESS HAS LEGS, KEEP ON RIDING IT

Overwhelming competition from FrontPage was a setback, and we had to shut down our CD-ROM operation. But we were convinced by now that the Internet was giving legs to the idea of a small-business network—tens of thousands of legs, in fact. Where those legs have taken us—and *will* take us in the future—is a big story. While the story began at the end of the twentieth century, it has most fully unfolded, blossomed—hell, *exploded*—in the twenty-first century, as Fran Tarkenton Small Business Network became GoSmallBiz.com, one of the three core businesses that make up Tarkenton Companies today.

So let me pick up the GoSmallBiz story in the next chapter, which carries us into the still-new century. But before we leave the 1990s, I do want to tell you how another of our current core businesses came into being. It's important because, whereas KnowledgeWare and GoSmallBiz were all about innovation in an environment of high-speed technological change, Teleconferencing Services LLC highlights the critical role that durable, "old-school" values play in that same high-speed environment.

We founded Teleconferencing Services in 1997, while FTSBN was just getting started. I'm not advising you to recklessly start one thing after another, but whenever I've had the means and the staff to juggle more than a few companies, I've done so. Even if you prefer to focus intensely on one thing at a time, never be so focused that you miss peripheral, unexpected opportunities or perils. Just because I was excited by the idea of helping small businesses didn't mean I had to close my eyes to everything else.

In 1997, through a business associate, I was introduced to Gary Nordheimer in Washington, D.C. We discovered we had a common interest in telecommunications, and, a short time later, Gary came to me with an idea for a tele-conferencing service. At the time, it was a little offbeat, because with personal computers and the Internet all the rage, telephone technology was about as sexy as the long gray beard of Alexander Graham Bell. But offering truly convenient, efficient, reliable, and secure multiparty conferencing was actually a business essential—especially for smaller firms that did not have major IT departments capable of setting up and running such calls.

Gary had terrific insight into two key customer categories: legal and financial firms. Typically, both types of firms were small, yet they dealt with high-value and/or high-risk matters in which speed, reliability, and security were of paramount importance. Serving these customers might not be sexy, but it was demanding. They needed the best technology available. That was a given, and it was also the easiest part of the product for any company to supply. Conferencing technology, even the best, was a commodity. Any competent provider could furnish it. The hard part, the part capable of differentiating one brand from another in this industry, was customer service. That is where Gary proposed to excel. He would provide dedicated service reps to his customers. He would ensure their responsiveness, and they, in turn, would ensure fail-safe reliability—overseeing a system that responded to outages *before* they affected the customer's call. Equally important, the system would be secure, adhering to or exceeding industry best practices. Gary also understood that legal and financial professionals customarily bill their clients by the clock. They therefore needed accurate and unimpeachable billing records for each teleconference. He had figured out how to provide precisely that.

I saw it right away. Gary's proposal joined cutting-edge technology, using multiple carefully vetted "conference bridge" providers, to a level of customer service that drew on enduring principles of customer satisfaction specifically tailored to the needs of each client. The latest technology would be joined to good old-fashioned values of personal service, absolute reliability, and transparent trust. This combination would provide us with price protection and differentiation in what was otherwise a high-tech commodity. We could become a distinct and distinctive *brand*. Technology, as I well knew, changed and changed fast. It could raise a company up, and then knock it over in a heartbeat. The human side of the value proposition, however—service, trust, transparency, accountability—endured.

A lot has happened since Teleconferencing Services started in 1998, including the development of all sorts of low-cost and even no-cost, do-it-yourself conferencing platforms like Skype, Google Hangouts, and GoToMeeting. Yet our company continues to thrive, because our customer base has remained loyal. Prices per minute have plummeted, but the minutes consumed have easily compensated for that.

Teleconferencing Services is a lesson in the value of uncompromising customer service. That value is of great strategic importance, but even the very best *strategy* is valueless if you fail to execute it on the day-to-day *tactical* level. Two executives, Brad and Rod Nordheimer, who happen to be Gary's sons, assumed primary responsibility for running the company. From the start, they were fanatical (and I mean that in the very best way) in their commitment to customer service. Their relentless execution of our high-value strategy has created enduring value for the brand.

And that brings me to something else about the role of old-school values in contemporary business. Right is right and wrong is wrong every day of the week. Recognizing this fact a few years back, I told Gary that we needed to redistribute our partnership. When we started the company, we divided ownership 50/50 between us. Now I proposed—and Gary instantly agreed—that the *four* of us each take a 25 percent stake. Brad and Rod had not asked for it, but both Gary and I knew it was the right thing to do. Their execution of our vision of high-value customer service drives the company's longevity in an environment of rapidly changing technology. Yet again, culture trumps everything, even the relentless cycle of innovation and failure. And when you have the right culture, the culture that *works*, giving away half your stake to make sure it keeps on going turns out to be an unbeatable bargain.

CHAPTER 5

WORK, LEARN, INNOVATE, EXECUTE

THINK OUTSIDE THE PLAYBOOK

CONTINUALLY ADD VALUE

IN A WORLD OF CHANGE, TAKE THE LONG VIEW

START LEARNING, KEEP LEARNING

One of the original owners of the Minnesota Vikings was H. P. Skoglund, who grew up in northern Minnesota—humble origins in a tough, cold place—started an insurance company, and built it into a huge success. Bemidji is a Minnesota town famous for three things: giant statues of mythical lumberjack Paul Bunyan and his blue ox Babe, a passion for the sport of curling, and some of the coldest temperatures in the United States. (I believe it snowed every month but July.) Our training camp was up there, and it was in Bemidji that I first met Mr. Skoglund, who showed up in person to meet with the brand-new team he co-owned.

"The harder I work," he told us with a smile, "the luckier I get." H. P. was a great owner and a great man who built a wonderful business and helped a lot of people. No wonder those words have stuck with me ever since I first heard them.

Professional football players travel a lot, and that means they fly a lot. When I was in the NFL, most of the guys used their flight time as downtime, a time to zone out or take a nap. Me? The harder I work, the luckier I get. I would pull down my tray table, pull out a pad of paper, and draw formations—innovative formations, crazy formations, unheard-of formations, one after the other. I was noodling, experimenting. It was something I had been doing forever. When I was a kid, I collected bubble-gum cards—all the professional football players and all the college players. I would take those cards and arrange them in different formations. Of course, I always saw to it that my team won, but my thinking—my strategic, tactical, innovative thinking—began with moving those cards around, offense against defense. By the time I got into high school, the cards were long gone, and my habit of doodling formations with pen and paper took over. It followed me through college and into the NFL. It was always my way of expanding my horizons as a quarter-back by opening up all the possibilities of eleven on eleven in a field fifty-two by a hundred yards. Within these con-straints, how could I position my people to get an advan-tage over the other eleven people identically constrained? I laid out problems, and I solved them. Because I'm no genius, many—in fact, most—of my "solutions" never got beyond that pad of paper. Did that mean I was wasting my flight time in failure after failure? No! I was *invest-ing* that time in "failure," figuring out what deserved to get off the pad and onto the field and—even more important—what did not. Tom Edison discovered ten thousand materials that did not work as lightbulb filaments. I bet you that I discovered at least ten thousand formations that will not contribute to winning a football game. Valuable knowledge!

If you love to work, you can work any time. That's true whether you play football or clock in nine to five. Why limit your creativity to a few hours on the field or at a desk? The harder I work, the luckier I get. In the clubhouse, I watched hour on hour of game film. I also did what no other quarterback did back then. I talked with our defensive coaches: *If I do this, how would you defend against me?* My aim was to innovate, not just use and reuse the same old "tried-and-true" formations everyone already knew. Very early in my pro career, I was calling the plays myself. By the time I was twenty-five, I was doing a lot of the team's offensive thinking.

I'm still always thinking about how I can position my team for success. As an entrepreneur, that has always been the question that defined my most essential task. On the field or behind a desk, it's a quarterback's question, a leader's task. With the Fran Tarkenton Small Business Network, I began by asking how I could help small-business people position their enterprises for success. I learned that 70 percent of all business owners were sole proprietors and 90 percent of all businesses in America had one to ten employees. I also learned that the members of this vast segment of American enterprise—a half million start-ups every month!—had nowhere and nobody to turn to for vital business services and knowledge. If anything, a lot of them were getting scammed chasing one biz op after the next.

As the twentieth century came to an end, small-business people were being talked at by hucksters and motivational speakers. Endlessly. Tens of thousands were being recruited into network marketing schemes, which had a turnover of maybe 90 percent or more, as aspiring entrepreneurs dropped out after realizing they had bought into a dead end. Big meetings, loud music, the relentless beating of a hollow drum. A lot of noise, but no one to give them access to the knowledge and services small-business owners really and urgently needed.

Small business, I saw, was a vast market that was underserved, poorly served, not served, or shamefully abused. The big banks wouldn't talk to small-business operators. Management consultants were way out of their price range. Vendors of all kinds would deal with them on the crappiest of retail terms, if at all. Discouraging? Well, despite the noise, the hype, the vacuum of real value, most small-business people soldiered on, refusing to surrender. The indomitable spirit I saw and heard when I talked to them was inspiring.

By the time I was done with my self-assigned national listening tour, I felt I had earned a PhD in small business. I now *knew* these people. Knowledge, however, is never an end. It's always a start. It's not a guarantee of success. It's a start that positions you more advantageously for success, but by no means delivers it—no more than the time I invested in drawing football formations on long airplane rides guaranteed that my team would win. But make no mistake, it did nudge the odds in our favor.

Now that I knew what small businesses and the people who ran them were all about, I could start to build a business to help them. I saw that while the hucksters were selling them silver bullets hollow at the core—one "surefire" biz op after another—so many small-business people were nevertheless still willing to try and to fail and to try again. They seemed to me downright heroic. What if I could connect them with products, services, and knowledge they could actually use? Unlike the hucksters, I wouldn't promise, let alone guarantee, success. But I would offer to help them fail better, faster so that the odds of their succeeding would be so much better.

THINK OUTSIDE THE PLAYBOOK

Why not simply stow your tray table, recline your seat, and sleep away all those air miles? Why not just memorize the playbook you've been given and leave it at that? Why innovate? Why invent? Why squander downtime doodling and noodling and learning more if all the answers you need are between the covers of the playbook? Who's paying you for all that extra work? If you can't monetize it, why not just unplug and get some shut-eye?

Here's a short answer to these questions: if you take a nap after memorizing the playbook, you'll never get any better than the playbook, which, by the way, becomes increasingly obsolete with each day that goes by, as your opponents learn your moves. But here's an even shorter answer: unconsciousness is no fun.

Knowledge is a start, not an end. The more you learn, the more you try. The more you try, the more you fail. The more you fail, the more you question. The more you question, the harder you work. The harder you work, the luckier you get. And what could be more fun than being lucky?

Too many businesspeople seek out every silver bullet, from two-day, $5,000 You Can Do It! seminars to two-year, $100,000 MBA programs, in a bid to grab hold of the holy knowledge, the final answers, the Great Unabridged Playbook. I saw this when I started FTSBN: charismatic hucksters were preying upon mom-and-pop businesspeople with daylong or two-day "seminars" promising overnight success. At least two things were—and still are—wrong with such programs. First and invariably, they were the work of pitchmen who had never run a small business. Second, no life, no career, is fundamentally changed by a day or two spent listening to someone in a hotel ballroom. Rome wasn't built in a day, and neither was any viable business. The seed of FTSBN and GoSmallBiz was our desire to offer an alternative to disappointment and deception.

Let me add an important point here. Small-business operators are not the only people vulnerable to the promise of a sovereign secret revealed. The leaders of many big, established businesses see their brand as *their* silver bullet.

They worship their brand as something sacred, ultimate, and absolute. In such enterprises, innovation inevitably gives way to pointless meetings, high-priced corporate retreats, and the publication of an annual report that is a combination of excuses based on a "challenging" economy (or bad weather or whatever) and self-congratulation based on nothing much at all.

True knowledge is a start, not an end. It is a question, not an answer. When Walmart's Sam Walton or Home Depot's Bernie Marcus sought meaningful and productive knowledge, they did not attend a seminar, assemble a committee, convene a board meeting, or worship at the altar of their brand legacy. They asked questions, directly, here and now. When they wanted to know what products and services their customers wanted and needed—here and now—they actually *asked* them. And by "asked them," I mean they got up, got out, asked, listened, and then acted. And how do I know this? Both Sam Walton and Bernie Marcus told me because *I* asked them.

Bernie Marcus, for instance, told me how he once approached a customer in a Home Depot parking lot who had a pallet of lumber. Bernie said to him, "I see you've got all that lumber. Where're the nails?"

"Nails are no good here," the customer replied.

"No good?"

"No. I buy the lumber here and just go down the street for the nails."

Bernie went into the store and walked up to the hardware department manager.

"Ralph, are we selling many nails?"

"Not as much as we used to."

"Why?"

"We changed vendors. The new nails—they bend."

By asking questions, Bernie learned that the nails his stores sold were failing. He didn't convene a meeting or form a committee to investigate the failure. He acted on it immediately by making certain that they changed vendors—again. He made it happen.

Failure is a gift, but only if you know about it. You don't know unless you ask, and the people you ask are the customers and the people who work for you to serve the customers.

CONTINUALLY ADD VALUE

As we began to build the company that became GoSmallBiz, we asked questions: Who is our market? What do they need? How can we help them?

They were thoughtful questions. But no matter how thoughtful your questions, the answers are only as good as the sources you go to for answers. Rick Gossett and I identified and met with a long list of companies that also wanted to reach out to small businesses. In addition to Dun & Bradstreet with its Business in a Box, we met with Intuit, Frontier Communications, Sprint, Federal Express, Humana/Employers Health, Netscape, Hertz, OfficeMax, Sir Speedy, Kinko's, Mail Boxes Etc., Coca-Cola Company, and Charles Schwab. We knew from our experience with IBM that partnerships could accomplish great things, and so we struck upon the idea that we would aggregate products and services from each of our partners and that each of our partners would bring us customers to purchase the "box."

In theory, it was a terrific idea. In practice, however, too many of our potential partners were very interested in taking. In giving? Not so much. This is when we realized that we had to move beyond selling nothing but a box of discounted services for a one-time price of ninety-nine dollars. The box got us into the game. It got us *doing*, and that was a terrific thing, because actually taking action is the best way to start and build a business. The box approach hadn't failed, exactly, but it wasn't exactly working, either.

We had to do more. If we were to fulfill our mission to help small businesses, to be a place where small-business people could access everything they needed, to be the go-to center of a small-business community, we had to offer more than discounts and tools. And we also had to offer more than cut-and-dried information.

I was in Dallas, Texas, knocking on doors in an effort to promote FTSBN and appearing as a guest on a business-oriented TV show, when I learned about a company called Pre-Paid Legal Services Inc. (PPL). Unlike the other companies we had met with in search of partnerships, PPL was hardly a corporate giant. Back in the 1990s, it was a small, struggling firm based out of Ada, Oklahoma, selling individuals and families unlimited access to professional legal counsel in almost all fifty states for a flat fee of between seventeen and twenty-one dollars a month.

If the high cost of legal services could be a serious problem for the average American family, it was an even graver problem for small businesses, which were even more likely to need legal assistance. What, then, if we could offer our customers affordable access to legal services, the small-business equivalent of PPL's "family plan"?

We had thought about working with firms in Atlanta as the basis for a small-business legal product, but the lowest cost we could find was one hundred to two hundred dollars per hour. Small businesses couldn't afford that! PPL's seventeen to twenty-one dollars a month for a lawyer sounded better and better to us. In fact, it sounded too good to be true.

"Gee," I said to Rick, "what the hell kind of lawyers can you get to work for seventeen dollars a month?" Rick had already started the due diligence and responded that the provider law firms were all A-rated.

So I called Harland Stonecipher, founder and CEO of Pre-Paid Legal, invited him to Atlanta for a meeting—and immediately ran up against another stumbling block. His idea was to sell *our* entire small-business product through *his* network marketing group, whereas my intention was to sell a pre-paid legal package as part of *our* product.

"Harland," I told him, "I don't know a thing about network marketing. Is that something like Amway?"

He chuckled and shook his head. So I made myself clearer.

"My understanding, Harland, is that network marketers are more about recruiting than selling products. They are recruiting machines, and I just don't see how we can make that work for us."

Now, Harland was obsessed with building his family legal-plan business. He had already tried to build a small-business version and failed. He just didn't *feel* a mission to build a product to help small businesses. What he saw in me—personally—was nothing more or less than a Hall of Fame football player–celebrity whose brand he could leverage to help him recruit more salespeople. But I liked the man, and while our interests diverged, I trusted him. We may not have come to each other with the same mission, but we were both men of integrity.

I made a deal to let Harland benefit from my brand, on condition that he agreed to allow us to train and certify every one of his salespeople who sold my brand. What is more, we would handle the marketing of our product, controlling it from our Atlanta office. He accepted and set out to design a version of the PPL family plan specifically tailored to the requirements of small businesses. In the meantime, we began training and certifying his people, and a new partnership was launched. In business, you can either hem, haw, talk, meet, create committees, and plan endlessly, or you can negotiate, learn, and act. Experience, the old saying goes, is the greatest teacher. If you fail, you at least learn, firsthand, what won't work—and that means you've learned what you need to fix. Harland and I wanted to work together. We therefore found a way to make the partnership succeed.

We did a trial run, and the results were indisputable. A few hundred customers became a few thousand. I make it a point, however, never to assume that an upward trend means sustained, let alone permanent, success. I continue to ask questions. Success is something you must interrogate.

Rick and I could see that the legal plan added real value to our business; we also could see that it was not enough to sustain our business. We needed to add even more value in order to earn the continuing business of our customers.

We turned to developing the idea of unlimited access to business consulting services. Massive consulting firms like McKinsey, Booz Allen, and Ernst & Young recruited armies of consultants and built huge infrastructures. Impressive—but this priced them far beyond what small businesses could pay. Eager to add consulting to our small-business value proposition, Rick, a CPA who had been a consultant with a practice specializing in small business, made me an offer I couldn't refuse. He volunteered his expertise and, for a brief time, was a one-man consultant army. As for infrastructure, we simply harnessed the go-to technology of the times (this was about 1998)—the fax machine. We invited our customers to fax their business- and accounting-related questions to our consulting service.

Rick was very good at answering questions—so good, in fact, that the faxes soon began flowing in at an alarming rate. This response was ample proof that our subscribers valued our customized consulting service, just as they valued customized legal consultation. We quickly expanded the consulting side of our business, tapping a wide variety of experts from around the country. Their fields of expertise ranged from technology to marketing to finance. And they were *real* experts, because they were experienced, seasoned businesspeople, not self-proclaimed authorities and coaches. Consulting became a bigger and bigger part of our "value proposition," quickly growing from zero to more than fifty thousand subscribers a month. All questions were submitted in writing, as were our responses to them. We promised a response within thirty-six hours, and each response was vetted by other staff members—we called it a "sanity check"—before it was sent to the subscriber. I am proud to say that virtually no one ever complained that they had received bad advice, let alone a wrong answer.

Adding customized, interactive services allowed us to change Fran Tarkenton Small Business Network from a ninety-nine-dollar unit of merchandise to a monthly subscription product, which was a far more scalable and sustainable business model precisely because it delivered greater value by providing more and more useful help. The advance of technology supercharged this transformation. As the late twentieth century transitioned into the twenty-first, we stopped using the fax machine as our consulting platform and bought into the Internet— all the way. The web became our platform, and Fran Tarkenton Small Business Network became the web-centric GoSmallBiz.com in 2001. Today, of course, the Internet supports hundreds of thousands—millions—of interest-based e-communities. GoSmallBiz was among the pioneers of this movement.

None of it happened by magic. The dot-com bubble that turned so many dot-coms into dot-bombs in the first couple years of the twenty-first century was the product of large numbers of companies and their investors simply hopping aboard the Internet Express. This is not what we did.

The Internet offered a new platform for us to deliver our services and make them known, and a new means to communicate with our customers, but the key was still to make the best product possible, *to add the most value.* That, in turn, meant making sure our business partner,

Pre-Paid Legal, was fully aware of the new opportunities and challenges for our business and the customers we served. I got into my Lear 35 determined to meet with PPL's sales associates all over the country, to personally educate them about precisely what we were offering small businesses. Those PPL associates became our first sales force.

IN A WORLD OF CHANGE, TAKE THE LONG VIEW

We added tremendous value to PPL, and their sales network added value to us. Harland's company not only sold a legal plan to our customers, but also sold our small-business consulting services to its ever-growing customer base. Our product was more expensive than the legal product, yet it delivered more revenue to PPL and created more loyalty among subscribers, who renewed at a very high rate.

Our rapidly increasing subscriber base proved that our customers enthusiastically responded to value. We understood that this was not the same as wanting to be sold more products. So we took the long view. Instead of trying to squeeze more profit from each "unit" sold, we injected more value into each unit. Our profit margin narrowed, of course, but the increase in customers and retention of customers more than made up for the extra cost. Over the years, we have leveraged technology and expanded the services we offer to include a free, informative five-page website, a really simple accounting app called "Track My Transactions," a suite of human resources (HR) apps, customer relationship management (CRM) software, and an app to simplify the labor of creating business plans. As for services, GoSmallBiz now offers resources to incorporate your business, do digital marketing for you, and manage your social media. We have also created partnerships with small business–friendly credit unions, with payroll processor ADP, and with Deluxe Corporation, the check printer and digital services company. These partnerships enable us and our partners to reach and help even more small businesses.

The more we listened to our subscribers, the more we discovered that their needs extended beyond tools and services. So we began producing content. We made videos of me talking about my entrepreneurial experiences or interviewing small-business people, authors, and experts in various fields. We posted articles and blogs written by me or others. And we provided links to valuable information sources. Soon, GoSmallBiz became such a prolific producer of small-business knowledge and best practices that we decided to create another entity, Tarkenton Institute, to focus on this aspect of our work. Anyone who surfs the web quickly realizes that the word *content* has a wide range of meanings—from truly valuable packages of remarkable insight down to so much digital filler and fodder. The Tarkenton Institute was set up to address the needs of small-business owners with specific and valuable content.

The content-creating work of the Tarkenton Institute has taken GoSmallBiz and me in a remarkable new direction, which I'll tell you about in just a moment. But I don't want to give the impression that we think of the Internet as nothing more than a platform for content distribution. It is, first and foremost, an interactive forum. That is what most differentiates Internet media from "old-fashioned" broadcast media. And so we invite GoSmallBiz subscribers as well as those who choose to become cost-free members of FranTarkenton.com and SmallBizClub (developed in partnership with Office Depot/OfficeMax) to go online with me twice a month on Google Hangouts with questions about starting a business and business in general.

These days, I do fifteen minutes of fresh video content every week in an online small-business mentoring program. I bring in small-business experts from places like Wharton, MIT, and elsewhere. I bring in entrepreneurs and small-business operators. I talk to them about new ways of thinking about business, small business especially. Every week! And the content is available whenever our subscribers want it and on whatever devices they favor.

START LEARNING, KEEP LEARNING

In recent years, GoSmallBiz has truly become an enterprise in education. The focus on informational content, shared experience, best practices, interactive forums, and online tutoring laid the groundwork for something that has been incredibly exciting to me.

On January 28, 2013, Jere Morehead was announced as the finalist to become the twenty-second president of my alma mater, the University of Georgia. The appointment came as a surprise to some. Professor Morehead is not a product of the Ivy League, but of Georgia's state universities. In 1973, he enrolled at Georgia State, and in 1980, when he was twenty-three, he was awarded a JD from the University of Georgia School of Law. After receiving his law degree, he served as an assistant U.S. attorney, and then joined the faculty of the Terry College of Business of the University of Georgia as assistant professor of legal studies. He has had a distinguished career at Georgia ever since and was the university's senior vice president for academic affairs as well as provost. His selection in 2013 made him the first Georgia president to be appointed from inside the institution since 1950.

I was at a Georgia football game in 2013, attending a ceremony inducting my Georgia teammate and great friend Pat Dye—you met him in chapter 1—into the Circle of Honor, a UGA Athletic Association program that pays tribute to extraordinary student-athletes and coaches. I was down on the sideline, having been there all afternoon. (I far prefer watching the game from that perspective to the "luxury" of a premium box!) After a time, I was joined on the sideline by the brand-new president.

"When you come to a game, Fran," President Morehead said to me, "you have a presence, an energy, the kids really respond to." Without segue, he continued: "I know you do a lot of work with small businesses. What I want to know is, how can we work together with our Terry College of Business?"

He came up with the idea. I was in the right place at the right time to hear about it. I could not help but flash back to that day in 1958 when I took the field against Texas. If you want to get hit in the head by opportunity, make sure you put yourself where opportunity is—not on the bench and not in a deluxe skybox, either.

I'm not saying I instantly knew what to do in response to the president's invitation. I didn't shoot back a proposal then and there. But I sure did recognize an opportunity. It was the weekend. By the time I walked into my office on Monday morning, I must have talked to ten or twelve friends about my exchange with the new president—and I mean *talked*, not *bragged*. I related the brief conversation to each, and then I asked, "What do *you* think?"

By the start of the workweek, I had a pocketful of opinions. I sat down with Rick and told him what happened and some of the things my friends had suggested.

"We need to have an entrepreneurial certificate program with the Terry College of Business at the University of Georgia," he said. Just like that: a complete, affirmative, declarative sentence. I warned you: I've never had an original idea in all my life. But I do know a great idea when I hear one, and I know how to make things happen. Not to mention, I know how to surround myself with good people.

Jere Morehead asked Charles Knapp, president emeritus of the university and interim dean of the Terry College, to meet with us to structure the deal. Chuck and President Morehead pulled together other key university stakeholders, and, on our side, we mobilized the Tarkenton Institute to work with a team from the Terry College to create the Tarkenton Certificate in Entrepreneurship—a one-hundred-hour course of study in six modules, starting with principles of entrepreneurship, then moving on to planning, funding, customer acquisition, financial and legal considerations, and, finally, operations. The program covers everything from developing an idea into a business to sales to marketing. We took our camera crew into the classroom and filmed Terry College faculty teaching these principles to MBA students. The certificate program that we launched in early 2015 offers an MBA-level experience, but at a fraction of the cost in cash and time.

There really is nothing else like it. At one extreme, a gaggle of gurus promise to change your life with a two-day seminar in exchange for five thousand of your dollars.

(The only feature of your life a two-day seminar will change is your bank account—by suddenly diminishing it.) At the other extreme, institutions such as Babson College, Harvard Business School, and Stanford University offer certificate programs—generally targeting Silicon Valley types who are looking for venture funding, and clocking in at between $12,000 and $15,000. Most entrepreneurs and people who run typical family businesses are priced way out of these. We offer our program for less than $1,000, and we even award some scholarships. The coursework is delivered online and on demand, using any device with a browser and speaker. It targets businesspeople who run enterprises with one to ten employees, the biggest category of small businesses—yet that is the very category educational institutions have almost universally overlooked or deliberately ignored. Until now.

With the University of Georgia partnership in place, I immediately set to work gathering additional partners, starting with ADP, the payroll people, and Deluxe Corporation, historically in the check-printing business, but, having adapted to technology, now a powerhouse in digital marketing. Both of these companies work vigorously to serve the small-business market, and both want to market the certificate program to their small-business customers. That's about half a million customers of *each* company. Malcolm McRoberts, the senior vice president of small-business services at Deluxe, asked me if we could create a mini-course that his company could offer customers as a loyalty reward, with the added bonus that if his customers liked the mini-course, they could proceed to the full certificate program at a discounted price.

I told him yes, and we delivered a full session to him within thirty days: three hours of engagement, including sixty-two minutes of video instruction, and it's free. Once again, not my idea. None of this was my idea. But I got it done. And getting it done is the most important thing an entrepreneur does. If you fail, you gain the knowledge to try again and to get it done better. That is how we started with a small-business "box" and ended up with a small-business community and an entrepreneurial program with a great university. If that box had been a runaway success, we would never have gotten to something so much better—better business for us, and a far better value for the small-business community we serve.

CHAPTER 6

MISSION STATEMENT

NEVER LET A GOOD IDEA GET AWAY

GO INTO BUSINESS FOR YOURSELF
TO SERVE OTHERS

FORGET FOREVER, BE IN THE MOMENT,
LOOK TO THE FUTURE

MIND YOUR BUSINESS

THERE ARE JUST TWO UNFORGIVABLE FAILURES

believe that our partnership with the University of Georgia will be a financially rewarding business, and I have absolutely no doubt that it is a *good* business. It will bring income and added prestige to the university and its business school. It will help untold thousands of entrepreneurs to succeed—by giving them the knowledge they need to fail better, faster so that they can innovate and grow instead of suffering the slow decline of the status quo. In short, the partnership will make the world a better place.

If you have ever talked with a novelist, playwright, or scriptwriter or even taken a high school or college lit course, you've probably heard about something called a "character arc." The idea is that the lead character in a story starts out in one place and ends up in another, his or her experience forming between these two points the "arc" that is the action of the story. If the story I have been sharing with you ended right here, with GoSmallBiz and the Tarkenton Certificate in Entrepreneurship, the result would be a very neat arc. After all, everything I have done that has meant anything at all to me has involved learning and helping others to learn. But my life and my work are not a story. They are my life and my work, and they keep on going.

NEVER LET A GOOD IDEA GET AWAY

Maybe I could sell more copies of this book if I just called it "Secrets of a Successful Entrepreneur." The thing is, there's nothing secret about it. I concluded a speech I gave not long ago by saying, "The mission of business is the same as the mission of life. We're here to serve others." If *that's* a secret, it's one wide-open secret!

I mentioned earlier that there are three businesses at the core of Tarkenton Companies today. Teleconferencing Services is one, and GoSmallBiz and its related enterprises another. The third is Tarkenton Financial, a business that shares our corporate mission of serving others by helping them improve their lives. It's based on a great idea, but also on a corporate failure that provided us with an opportunity. Sometimes the gift of failure comes from someone else, in this case a soon-to-be fallen giant.

Tarkenton Financial began like this. Arthur Andersen LLP—before getting swallowed up in the infamous downfall of Enron, for which it served as auditor—was a blue-chip financial consultancy and one of the so-called Big Five accounting firms. Among the many products Andersen offered was an employee-assistance program called Financial Lifeline, sold to corporate human resources departments. Jim Sullivan ran the program for Arthur

Andersen and took it over entirely when Andersen decided to drop it. Financial Lifeline just wasn't working for them. Cut loose along with his program, Jim suddenly found himself with a small business to run. He came to us for help, asking that we introduce him to our partner Pre-Paid Legal and its network sales force.

After meeting with Jim, Rick Gossett and I realized that a relationship with Pre-Paid Legal was not a viable path for Financial Lifeline. But we liked Jim and the notion of offering some form of financial help–based product.

Just because an idea fails to produce a runaway success for one individual or company does not mean it isn't a good idea. Financial Lifeline looked to me like a good idea, and I believe in never letting a good idea get away. So, in 2001, Rick and I worked with Jim to create a business that offered the Financial Lifeline product to companies that would then sell it to retail customers as part of a service portfolio.

The redesigned business made money for us, but it failed to make as much money as we all thought it should. That failure encouraged us to keep working on it, and Rick made regular trips to Chicago to help Jim find a way to improve it. During one of those visits, Jim got a call from a man who wanted to add Financial Lifeline to a health insurance package he offered to his individual and small-business customers. Rick agreed to meet with the man at O'Hare International, before his return flight took off for Atlanta.

"So I'm at O'Hare," Rick tells the story today, "and, sure enough, this guy, Steve Lewit, shows up. I didn't expect much, but I had to respect his determination, and I gave him my full attention. Amazingly enough, as I listened, I found myself thinking: *You know what? This guy's got a brain. He's got some ideas that make sense.* So I extended a real invitation, asking him to come down to Atlanta for a proper meeting."

Uppermost on *Steve's* agenda was getting us into the health insurance business. We had no interest in that, because that was *big* business, with a complex infrastructure and bureaucracy, and while we had built a big business before, we much preferred establishing small, manageable businesses where our teams could be in constant personal contact with us. Being willing to try and to fail does *not* mean you have to risk failing at something you never wanted to do in the first place!

But Lewit mentioned he was also selling fixed annuities to individuals who were retired or planning for retirement. Rick realized that *this* business, distributing insurance-based annuities, was a much better fit with our culture than jumping into the health insurance industry.

The idea of selling annuities that removed some of the risk of retirement investment portfolios appealed to me. It was a business that could make people's lives better, making their retirement savings more secure. That was the sort of positive impact I like to make with my businesses, and I thought we could make money at it, which is important, because money is the fuel for the engine of getting things done.

We decided that the best way to proceed was to contract with insurance companies that had the best and most appropriate financial services for retirees, and then offer those services through our own trained network of independent insurance agents. I did have a history with the insurance industry. While I was attending the University of Georgia, I was a business major with a concentration in insurance. During my sophomore, junior, and senior seasons as a Georgia Bulldog, I worked for the Franklin Life Insurance Company—young as I was, I had earned my agent's license—selling the "President's Passbook Investment Plan" to my fellow students as well as door-to-door in Athens. I made enough to pay my fraternity dues and buy a car—a car people mistakenly assumed the football program had simply given me!

I gave up the insurance business when I was drafted by the Vikings, but during the 1970s, while I was running Behavioral Systems Inc., helping the textile industry improve productivity and competitiveness by training plant managers, the subject of insurance resurfaced. As you may remember from chapter 2, I had built a strong working relationship with Bury Hudson, HR director for Cannon Mills. Bury had explained to me then that textile employees had no company-sponsored pension or retirement plan and no insurance other than a feeble debit insurance scheme. The two of us agreed that creating something better would not only go a long way toward reducing the high employee turnover that was crippling Cannon and the entire southern textile industry, it was also the right thing to do. We agreed to institute a payroll-deduction insurance plan for all employees, guaranteed issue, no health questions asked, with coverage up to three times an employee's salary. Rates would be the best available. The lowest-paid mill floor worker would get the same terms as an executive. Predictably, it wasn't easy finding an underwriter, but I secured a deal with a solid company out of Nashville, and we launched the plan.

It was an instant hit, a huge success at Cannon, and I soon took it to other companies. While still running Behavioral Systems Inc., I built a pretty big insurance company, which I eventually sold.

The financial success felt great, naturally. But helping the textile industry and its workers—giving them a measure of real value and real security—felt even better. So, years later, the idea of using my brand to offer seniors and those approaching that age—"my people"—low-risk, insurance-based retirement products excited me. How did I begin? You probably guessed it. I talked to people, and I asked questions. I traveled to the existing wholesalers of retirement annuities. They were, I admit, impressive operations—impressive, that is, in the way that large, well-oiled factories are impressive. Their managers spoke less about helping their customers than they did about creating more and more customers. As for issuing policies, that was a process they routinely called "production." The industry standard that I saw reminded me of what I already knew about network marketing. It was all about recruiting more agents to "produce" more customers.

I wasn't interested in doing that. Not only did the world *not* need another insurance factory doing the same exact thing as the existing factories, it was not the way I wanted to do business. I was determined to innovate by putting the emphasis on service, on genuinely helping others by offering a high-value product in a high-value way.

"We're not going to be a factory," I told Rick. "We are going to be a five-star boutique hotel. We aren't going to recruit an army of thousands of agents, we are going to build a team of a few hundred: people we like, people we know. We are going to find and train agents with the right skills and right ethics. We will treat them like family, and we will provide them with the best technology and marketing tools."

My idea was to leverage my brand—my celebrity and reputation for integrity—to create a portfolio of trusted products. We would continue to earn that brand's good name every day by building and working with a team that shared our values. This included the insurance underwriters with which we contracted and the independent agents who came on board with us.

So Tarkenton Financial began in 2003. From the start, we offered retirement income planning based not on inherently risky securities, but on advanced insurance products, including fixed indexed annuities and indexed universal life insurance. Day to day, the business works this way: on the supply side, we contract with all the major A+ insurance companies, and, on the distribution side, we go out and selectively recruit independent insurance agents, individuals we consider elite professionals within the industry. They are a team—*our* team. I get to know each of them personally. They are paid by the insurance providers, who also pay us. We, in turn, give our agents the benefit of our brand and we back them with our product support, marketing support, training, and—not least of all—technology.

While the core of this business is founded on ethics, transparency, accountability, and personalization—the indispensable components of trust—we are not an old-fashioned company. We want our agents to have the kind of cutting-edge Internet presence that is essential both to service and to creating credibility in today's connected world. As in our other businesses, we put technology at the service of our core values. We have an IT staff that supports and assists our team in such areas as search engine optimization, site optimization, and social media—the elements of contemporary digital marketing.

As you saw in chapter 5, GoSmallBiz is a very web-centric company, and Tarkenton Financial benefits from the technological expertise and resources we have developed in web-based business. We have created and staffed in our Atlanta offices a state-of-the-art video production studio that produces video content for GoSmallBiz and that also supports Tarkenton Financial agents by creating professional-grade visuals for their websites and social media presence. We work with our agent partners to produce commercials and educational videos. In addition, we support our agent network with software tools, such as analytics that help agents identify and illustrate their clients' financial requirements for retirement, compare offerings from among all leading carriers, and generally facilitate decision making. In short, we make our money by providing our clients with the best services we can offer, services that successfully fill our clients' needs.

GO INTO BUSINESS FOR YOURSELF TO SERVE OTHERS

I've never started any business with the intention of making a quick buck and then shutting it down. That is a waste of time and effort, and it's not fair to anybody, not to customers or to employees. That's *not* the way to fail. The quick-buck approach puts the entrepreneur's reputation—my reputation—at risk. It does not accomplish *the mission* of business, which is to help and serve others. So I don't do it. Yet I *do* always recognize and accept the possibility that something I try will fail and maybe even fail sooner rather than later. If the business is worth trying, the prospect of failure, painful as it might be, I nevertheless see as a gift, because I know it will teach me something of value. In contrast, I don't know of any quick-buck, bound-to-fail business that has anything valuable to teach—except, maybe, a lesson in Don't Do This Again.

Some failures are swift and total—witness Scrambler's Village. Usually, however, a venture does not so much fail as it just does not work out well enough to create a sustainable business, or a business worth sustaining. In some ways, the sudden and total failure is easy. The question "Should I walk away now?" answers itself in these cases because you are left with little or no choice. The decision is made for you. Deciding to walk away from a venture that is eking out a small profit but just isn't everything you hoped it would be is actually much more difficult. And if you let emotional attachment to your "baby" take control, the decision can become downright impossible. It's a tough lesson, but we all need to learn to regard starting *and* stopping any *particular* business as a normal and necessary part of doing business in *general.* I've called it quits on a number of businesses, but I've never stopped doing business.

Tarkenton Financial did not begin with any grand plan. It started with ideas brought to me by others. Effective entrepreneurs look at all ideas that appear to promise opportunity, but they and they alone make the final decision about which ones to actually run with. In my case, the ideas that would blossom into Tarkenton Financial meshed perfectly with my own history and values. Going into insurance in a big-factory, high-production way might have been the most obvious path. But it was not right for me. What you decide to do must, first and last, be right for you. I believe our products and services are grounded in enduring business principles, namely the aim to help people, to improve their lives, and to earn their trust. Each agent we recruit is a team member. My objective is to give each of them the training and support they need to be the very best agent they can be. In this, it is no different from the way I approached my role as a football quarterback.

I always hope that each of the partnerships I build will last a long time. The best way to enter into a partnership is with the fullest possible measure of good faith. Yet both partners need to accept that a time may come to alter or to end their relationship. We eventually had differences with Steve Lewit that required ending our partnership. We made him a buyout offer, and he accepted it without rancor. Was it therefore a bad partnership, a mistake, a failure? Not at all. It resulted in a wonderful business.

We ended the partnership with mutual respect and honor. Similarly, when one of our independent agents proves incapable of meeting our standards or decides that we no longer benefit him or her, we part ways, and we try to do so with respect and without hard feelings. The fact is that you cannot control your partners or your employees. You can and must make your best effort to put them in a position to succeed for themselves and for the company. You can educate, train, provide constructive feedback on performance, and invite feedback in return. You can do everything possible to help partners and employees be the best partners and employees *they* can be. On one occasion, one of my Tarkenton Financial managers complained to me about an agent's failure to be honest with him. He was deeply upset, and I took him aside.

"Have you been up front and honest with *him*?" I asked.

"Yes."

"Have you been clear about what you need and expect from him?"

"Yes, I have."

"Have you asked what *you* can do for him? What *you* can do better?"

"I have," he answered.

"Then you have done all that you can do—all that can be done. The rest is up to him. If it doesn't work out, it's time to end the relationship, and to do so professionally and without any emotion except maybe your best wishes for his future somewhere else."

The best partnerships create satisfying feelings, but they are, first and last, business agreements. When problems arise, solve them in a clean, fair, humane, and honorable way. But solve them. You may be inclined to judge the end of a relationship a failure, but like all failures it is an opportunity to learn—on both sides. In any case, if you believe that "success" must be something that lasts forever, you will never enjoy success. *That* I can guarantee!

FORGET FOREVER, BE IN THE MOMENT, LOOK TO THE FUTURE

I know that not every partnership I enter into and every business I start is destined for longevity, much less forever, but every one of them is important to me. I *am* tempted to regard GoSmallBiz—together with the Tarkenton Certificate program—and Tarkenton Financial as more than just "important." To me, they are very special because, in them, I feel I have not only created profitable enterprises but have fully realized my intention of helping others and making a positive impact on the world we share.

Most of us go "into business for ourselves" precisely because we want to go into business *for ourselves* as opposed to working for a boss or an owner or a bunch of stockholders. But my experience has taught me that the best reason for going into business *for yourself* is to make life better *for others*. Making other people's lives better will determine whether your business will be profitable and a success, both financially and in terms of your own personal satisfaction.

Making other people's lives better is a business and life mission that serves the moment while investing in the future. At the beginning of this chapter, I quoted myself: "The mission of business is the same as the mission of life. We're here to serve others." Well, please forgive me, but I'm proud of having said it. It was part of a speech I gave to about eighteen thousand members and advisors of DECA, who were gathered in Atlanta's Georgia Dome for the organization's 2014 International Career Development Conference opening session. DECA had honored me with its Entrepreneurial Spirit Award and accorded me the privilege of delivering the keynote address at the conference.

DECA is a nonprofit that prepares high school and college students for success as entrepreneurs and business leaders. The organization is active in all fifty states and has more than 220,000 participants. I had been introduced to DECA in the spring of 2014 when Ellis Mass, a VP at Office Depot, asked me to keynote DECA's international convention. My speech was on Saturday night. Sunday I spent mentoring an impressive group of DECA students. These students blew me away with their ability to articulate their business ideas and ask meaningful questions.

If these young men and women are the future, I thought, *I want to invest in them, to help them, and to serve them.*

So, after the convention, *I* started asking questions— about DECA's mission and its base of support. Marriott, Men's Wearhouse, and Piper Jaffray were major supporters, which was great, but I was convinced that the organization deserved a much broader range of financial support from a much larger number of major corporate partners. I phoned John Fistolera, DECA's assistant executive director. I wanted to become a rainmaker for DECA and asked him how I could help. He came back with a plan for "Tark Tank." Students would compete in drawing up business plans. Corporate sponsors would then choose some of the best of these students and mentor them over the course of a school year, guiding them in refining their business plans and coaching them on presentation skills. The competition would culminate at DECA's International Career Development Conference, with the top three contestants earning a right to participate in a "Business Incubator" that would be managed by my team of small-business strategists, consultants, and marketers.

I loved the idea of Tark Tank and shared it with corporate leaders. I also hosted a luncheon at Atlanta's College Football Hall of Fame for key executives from ten major corporations I had identified as potential sponsors. They were excited, and they plan to sponsor teams in the debut "Tark Tank" competition.

Thanks to DECA, I've added a new mission to my life: getting more companies involved in nurturing the next generation of American entrepreneurs.

MIND YOUR BUSINESS

Helping others, serving others, solving the problems of clients and customers—that's what entrepreneurship is all about. Make no mistake. Making money is *necessary* to business, but despite what the hedge fund managers and venture capital "operators" might tell you, making money is not the *purpose* of business.

If you achieve the *real* purpose of business, if you help others—your partners and your customers—by delivering extraordinary value, then you will create the relationships and the trust that will build your business, and as a byproduct of this higher pursuit, you will make money. But money is a byproduct, not the point. That's why decades ago, the great author George Gilder devoted an entire book, a classic, titled *Wealth and Poverty*, to showing that capitalism, business, entrepreneurship is driven not by selfishness, not by greed, but by *altruism*, by giving, because before any entrepreneur makes money he has to create a product that makes someone else's life better.

Let me give you an example that's close to home. In recent years, fast-food restaurants have been pummeled. Customers are turning away from the empty calories, the disappointing taste, the poor value, and the lackluster service. An exception to this downward trend is Chick-fil-A, which the late S. Truett Cathy built into a national company that pulled down revenues of $5.1 billion in 2013 and contributed to Cathy's reported $4.2 billion personal net worth. I can't tell you whether Mr. Cathy set out to get rich, but I can tell you two things. First, yes, obviously, he got rich. Second, inside each of his stores is a sign that quotes him: "Food is essential to life; therefore, make it good." There is no sign that says "Food is essential to life; therefore, make money from it." His 1,800 stores, whether owned by the company or by franchisees, are closed on Sundays—typically a big day for fast-food restaurants—because he believed his employees should be encouraged to spend time with their families and attend church. (He did not compel them to do either.) He created a management system that treats employees as associates, giving them a path to promotion. For franchisees, ownership of one or more restaurants has proved to be a path to entrepreneurial success. With Ken Blanchard, Cathy wrote a book titled *The Generosity Factor: Discover the Joy of Giving Your Time, Talent, and Treasure.*

If your only mission in life and business is to make money, you risk two things.

First, in this narrow pursuit, you may very easily lose your soul—whatever "soul" means to you. To me, *soul* speaks of the highest human values: respect, trust, empathy, and love. It's true these values don't show up as line items on a balance sheet, but they're there all the same, and they show up in your life and ultimately in your business.

Second, if your main mission is to make money for yourself, you will probably fail. Not because somebody up there is punishing you, but because no customer or potential customer cares whether *you* make money. Of course you care. But, by definition, business is never a solo act. It requires people—plural—to exchange value for value. *You* need to provide *value* for money. If you focus exclusively on getting money, you're focusing exclusively on yourself. If you do that, don't be surprised if you don't get anywhere. But if you focus on creating value for others, you have a fair

chance of receiving value in return. The thing is, "value"—
sustainable value—cannot be reduced to dollars and cents.
It is far more meaningfully defined in terms of making
someone else's life better. The more you multiply this value,
the more successful your business and your life.

THERE ARE JUST TWO UNFORGIVABLE FAILURES

In this book, I've tried to make the point that success
doesn't come from some secret elixir, but is the result of
learning from failure, which properly understood is not an
end but a means to better things. In the process, I've tried
to share what I've learned from long experience. Clearly, I
do not have all the answers, but, despite what they might
tell you, no one else does either. Gurus with all the answers,
who offer silver bullets, "one-minute" solutions, and two-
day seminars, are making promises that are impossible to
keep. If you want answers, you'll find them by study, by
experience, by doing, by asking endless questions, and most
especially by learning from mistakes.

But while there is no secret of success, there is a secret
of failure—namely that failure is a gift. It is a gift that

keeps us from the slow death that is the status quo, the delusion that what worked yesterday will therefore work tomorrow. Clinging to the status quo has never been a safe bet, because while there are eternal values—values that are essential to your business—life itself is about change, and technology has accelerated the inevitability of change. So take a chance. Do something. Fail at it. Learn from it. Try again.

Failing to try is one of only two unforgivable failures. All the other types of failure, except for one I note below, are not only forgivable but worthy of celebration. Without failure, there would be no learning, no education, no progress. Without failure, there would be no innovation— because, wallowing in success, why would you ever want to change?

Without the need to learn, to change, to innovate, and to improve, there would be no reason to help yourself or others, to make your life or the lives of others better. In short, there would be no reason for anything but the most basic of businesses, nothing to motivate the creative, innovative exchange of value for value.

Fortunately for all of us, we succeed by trying, even if many of our attempts end up as failures. In business today, propelled as it is by the nearly frictionless technologies of digital interconnection, instant exchange, almost instant delivery, and as close to limitless access to goods and services as any civilization has ever enjoyed, everything, every opportunity, every failure, happens *faster*, but the potential for reward is even greater. Never has there been so much opportunity for entrepreneurs, for people with new ideas and new businesses. There is a constant demand for change, for improvement, for greater quality, for more variety, for better solutions, all driven by the failure of *previous* changes, improvements, and solutions. Failure drives innovation. So don't fear failure, accept it as a gift— the golden key that ultimately unlocks what works and delivers success.

But remember this too: all success is temporary unless you always put your customers first, remembering their needs, always improving on what you can offer them, always improving your business. To that end, you need to accept, forgive, and even welcome the failure that leads to innovation. Embrace technology, but do not worship it to the exclusion of everything else in business. Doing so is the only *other* unforgivable business failure I know of.

Today, you absolutely need technology to build your business, but you cannot build it on technology alone. Technology is necessary to business, but not sufficient. Even the enterprise most fiercely driven by technological innovation must also create and honor a culture of service, help, value, transparency, and respect—a culture of love, the love of customers, employees, investors, community, and society itself. Call it a culture of doing the right thing to make life better.

Such a culture and the values it embodies are as *unchanging* as innovation is *changing*. Yet those of us in business are not called on to choose between innovation and a culture of values. The two are totally compatible with one another. In fact, a culture of values gives us reason to innovate, to create better ways to improve people's lives by providing them with new products and services. Now more than at any other time in history, success requires innovation and, therefore, both the possibility and the reality of failure. Success, as much today as ever before, also requires creating and honoring a culture of enduring values. The mission of business *is* the mission of life. Take joy in both.

APPENDIX

TRANSCRIPT OF KEYNOTE ADDRESS TO DECA'S 2014 INTERNATIONAL CAREER DEVELOPMENT CONFERENCE

Hello there! How are we doing? Are you having any fun? [cheers] You know, I did play football with those big ol' ugly men you just saw on that [screen] for eighteen years. But what I really am, I'm an entrepreneur. I'm like what you are, and what you're studying, and what brings you here. And I think it's so super cool that you come to my hometown, you come here where the Atlanta Falcons play their football games, and you come here competing about business. Is that cool or not? [cheers] I mean, my gosh! Now, you'll probably have just a little bit of fun while you're here too, right? [cheers]

I played eighteen years in the National Football League. I was six feet tall, 185 pounds, and they didn't draft me in the first round. They didn't draft me in the first round or the second round; they drafted me in the third round, and the reason they did is because they didn't think I was big enough, strong enough, smart enough, good enough, to play. But it really doesn't matter how other people might judge you and think of you, and think of your potential, because they don't know what's in your heart and soul and how hard you're going to work and how dedicated you are. And you and I are in control of our destiny, and the people who didn't draft me weren't. Eighteen years later, I set every passing record there ever was in the National Football League, I won more games than any quarterback that ever played, I quarterbacked my team to three Super Bowls out of the first eleven. And then I told them as I left, eighteen years after I started, I said I'm six feet tall and 185 pounds, and I'm big enough to play in this league with all you big boys out there. [cheers]

People come to me and say, "You're a lucky guy, you made all of this money playing pro football, and you became a celebrity." Well, today they make a lot of money.

Peyton Manning makes $23, $24 million a year. Tom Brady makes $25 million a year. [cheers] Uh-oh, we've got some people from Boston here! [cheers] I came in to play for the Minnesota Vikings. [cheers] Go Vikings! I was on the very first team in Minnesota, in 1961. They were a new expansion team. I played in the first game they ever played. You want to hear what my salary was? Peyton Manning makes $23 million a year. LeBron James makes $30 million a year. I was a star, record-setting quarterback. I made $12,500 a year. [cheers] So I worked. I went out in the off-season and I worked. Let me tell you what a glamorous job I had. I met the young man here who is the head of DECA from a student standpoint, and he's from Sioux Falls, South Dakota. [cheers] When I was twenty-two years old, I was a star player in the National Football League, and I needed to make more than $12,500, so I got a job. And my job was to go out to South Dakota in January, and February—and it's cold out there—and my job was to knock on the doors of shipping clerks (so it's an outdoor job), and get them to ship their goods on Wilson Truck Systems, which was based in Sioux Falls, on their eighteen-wheelers—it was all regulated—from the Dakotas to Minnesota, Chicago, and back. That's how glamorous my job was! But they paid me a lot of money. Guess how much money they paid me? $600 a month.

I learned business by doing business. Farmers learn to farm by going out and farming. I've built twenty companies, I've worked for other companies, I've learned everything from other people. None of us has original thoughts. We learn from what we hear, what we see, what we read, so it's so important that we come to places like this and we see each other. You will learn from each other; you will learn from mentors here. The whole reason for leadership, successful leadership, successful life, is people that are curious. We have to ask questions. And then we have to listen. And we have to ask questions of everybody that we can find. I learned to play quarterback from talking to other quarterbacks, and talking to coaches, and talking to ex-quarterbacks, and that's how I learned. It's not about what your SAT score is, it's not what your grade point average is, it's not how big or small you are, it's not whether you're female or male, it's not any of that. It doesn't matter what state or country you're from. It's up to you. It's you being smarter every day. It's you reaching out and asking more questions every day, being more curious every day, and understand that the mission of business is the same as the mission of life. And what is that? To make money? No! The mission of business is to help people, to solve problems, to tell people the truth, to make the customer experience great, to produce products and services that help people, that solve problems, that make people better. And you know what people say to me? *No, that's not the mission of business. We read about the billionaires on Wall Street, and we hear all about people in high-tech making billions of dollars—the mission of business is to make money!* It's not. It's to help people. It's to be transparent. It's to tell the truth. It's to make the customer experience great and have products and services that make people better and solve problems. If that is your mission, you will have a sustainable mission, and the byproduct of that is that you will make money for your company or for your own company, whichever it might be. If your mission going in is to make money and to get rich, then people will hit you with biz ops—*We're going to make you rich; come do my deal; we'll make you a million dollars in two days.* If your mission is to make money going in, you'll compromise your principles.

And all you have to do is to read the *Wall Street Journal*'s and the *New York Times*' everyday business sections, and you'll see where people on Wall Street [end up].

There's a company called SAC, S-A-C. The owner of the company, Steven Cohen, is worth $9 billion. How do you make $9 billion by trading stocks? And the way he made $9 billion, well, they have convicted him down there of cheating and insider trading, so they are going to fine him $1.9 billion. That's not what it's about. It's about transparency. It's about doing the right thing.

And business and learning is a process, and it continues to be a process. And I'm going to give you a key to it all. Every day of my life from the time that I can remember to right now, I wake up with a sense of desperation. I want to go out and do something good. I want to go out and help somebody. I want to go out and give good advice. I want to go out and solve problems for people. And I wake up with a sense of desperation. And where did I learn that? Like most of my learning, it came from the football field.

I was a quarterback in Athens, Georgia, sixty miles from here. We won the state championship of all the schools [cheers]. Oh, Georgia, there we are! We won the state championship here, and all the colleges were recruiting me. But the only college that really wasn't recruiting me was my hometown of Athens, the University of Georgia Bulldogs! [cheers] And the reason they didn't recruit me was they had two quarterbacks they had drafted the year before who were great quarterbacks. They didn't need me. But the local people put pressure on them, and they took me, even though they didn't want me. Back in those days, the freshmen couldn't play football on the varsity team, so I didn't play until my sophomore year.

So as we came into my sophomore year, these other two quarterbacks, Charley Britt and Tommy Lewis, were number one and number two, and the coach said to me, "Fran, you're a great player and you're a great guy, and we want you to play for us down the road, but we're going to redshirt you," which means they're not going to play me, but I'd have an extra year of education. I said, "I'm going to graduate in four years, Coach. I think I can help your team, and I want to play right now, and I'm going to work real hard to change your mind when we come back in the fall." And I worked all summer, and I worked out, and I was ready to go. We came back in the fall, and were getting ready for the season, going through the practices, and I was better than these two guys! But the coach wasn't going to play me. He was going to redshirt me. And I was determined not to be redshirted. I didn't know what a sense of desperation was, but I had a sense of desperation.

Have you ever been to that point, when you knew you could do something but they wouldn't let you do it? They were holding me back.

We went out to Texas to play our first game, in Austin, Texas, against the Texas Longhorns. Any Texans in here? [cheers] And we went out to play those Texas Longhorns, and it's on Saturday night television, and there's seventy thousand people in the stadium, and there's lights, and I was nineteen years old, a sophomore, and I was so excited. But I wasn't going to play! I was going to sit on the bench all night! So we get out there on the field and start the game, and I didn't sit on the bench. Don't ever sit on the bench! I stood right next to our coach, Wally Butts, and I stood next to him all during the game, and I said, "I think Charley Britt's getting a little tired out there. He's limping. I think he's hurt; he hurt his leg. I need to go in there, Coach, and give him just a break. Just let me go in for one play." I bugged him the entire night.

We went through two and a half quarters. We're midway in the third quarter, we're behind 7 to nothing, and I'm really desperate. I've gotta get myself in. I don't know what to do. But they punt to us, and we have a guy who fair catches the punt on the 5-yard line. I'm standing on the 50-yard line. I look back here, and Charley Britt, the other quarterback who had been playing, he was sitting on the bench! I looked at him. I looked at all of the chaos on the field, the changing of players, and I bolted onto the field. I put myself in. I ran out on the field. I put myself in; the coach never saw me. [cheers] Later on, Charley Britt, the other quarterback, said, "You put yourself in? I thought he put you in." I said, "No, no, I put myself in." And I added, "Most of my errors are errors of assumption. Assume nothing; question everything. Too bad, Charley."

So I'm out on the field, and my teammates are saying, "What are you doing out here? You're supposed to be redshirted." And I say, "No, we're going to play." We start driving. We make a first down, we make two first downs, we make three first downs. We're at the 40-yard line. I look over at the coach, and I acknowledge him out there— he didn't blink. We go down to the 5-yard line. Now we're stymied. We're losing 7 to nothing. It's the fourth quarter of the game. It's now third down and 5 yards. We gotta score on this play, or we're done. So I call a pass play, and I came out, and Texas was really good. And they rushed the passer, and I ran to the right, and I ran to the left, then I circled back—and they call me a scrambler, you know—

and I ran more to the right, and finally, just before they tackled me, I threw the ball and hit our man in the end zone. He catches the ball, and we have a touchdown. Now the score is Texas 7, Georgia 6.

They put our extra point kicker on the field to tie the game with an extra point, but this was the first year we had the option to kick an extra point, like you do now, or go for two points. I waved—at nineteen years old—I waved the kicker off the field. I waved him off the field. [cheers] I tell our team, I say, "Now guys, we're going to go for two points. If we don't make it, you're going to fly back to Athens, Georgia, from Austin, Texas, but I'm going to have to take the bus. He'll never let me back on that plane again."

So I call another play, and I roll out to the right, circle back to the left, as I'm being rushed by their team. And I've got good news and bad news for you: I've got a guy wide open in the end zone. I got a six-foot-four, 210-pound end wide open in the end zone, but this end was named Gordon Kelly—he ended up being a linebacker in the National Football League—and he had hands of stone. If I threw him ten balls, he would drop nine. But he was open; I had no other choice. I said a little prayer, and I threw it, and I hit him right between the eight and the four. I mean, I threw him a perfect ball. And it hit his hands, went right through his hands, hit his chest, and started falling to the ground. I saw my life going away right then. I was cranking up that Greyhound Bus to go back to Athens, Georgia, because I wasn't going to get a seat on the plane. And I saw this big ol' six-foot-four guy. He crumbled to the ground, he fell to the ground, and he stretched out his long arms, and he caught it. [cheers]

Now, think about that in your life. Who's in control of your life? You are! Every morning, create a sense of desperation to get things done, to help people, and you have a better chance. I didn't know what desperation was then, but I know what it is now. And in that situation, if I don't take that move, I might never have played quarterback for Georgia again. I might still be sitting on the bench. That means I wouldn't have gotten drafted by the Minnesota Vikings, that means I wouldn't have set all the passing records in the National Football League. You make your breaks. Let me say that again: You make your breaks. And you're here in this great conference, this great competition, for the next two days. Talk to everybody. Ask questions of everybody. Get all of the knowledge and information you can, because life is a process. Whenever you think you've got all of the answers, you don't have any. Keep that process going. And continue to get better. And continue to learn. And remember this: The mission of business is the same as the mission of life. We're here to serve others. It's not about us. It's about our friends, it's about our partners, it's about our customers. God bless you.

ACKNOWLEDGMENTS

This book could not have been written without the help of my teammates. Alan Axelrod was an invaluable resource in listening to my stories and helping me organize them and give them context. Rick Gossett, my partner in each business that I undertake, is my sounding board and is willing to add a different perspective to my own thinking. Jill Blitch has been my administrative assistant throughout our mission to help small business. She handled the details and set up the calls and meetings and managed to keep the peace when everything changed. Lynda Bekore, whom I first met as producer of my weekly radio show, arranged interviews with authors and experts. Edwin Bevens, our in-house master of the written word, reviewed all of the many drafts. And finally, my good friend Mark Brown accepted my daily calls and listened as I developed my thoughts out loud.

INDEX